The
Nagasaki British Consulate
1859 to 1955

Brian Burke-Gaffney

FLYING CRANE
2019

BRIAN BURKE-GAFFNEY

All Japanese names are rendered in the Japanese fashion with the surname first.

For Taka and Saya,
frontrunners in the vanguard of history and culture

CONTENTS

INTRODUCTION

When the Dutch galleon *De Liefde* foundered on the shore of Bungo (present-day Oita Prefecture) in 1600, William Adams, pilot on the ill-fated ship, became the first Briton to set foot in Japan. The native of Gillingham, Kent went on to serve as an advisor to Shogun Tokugawa Ieyasu and to help the English East India Company establish a factory (trading post) at Hirado in present-day Nagasaki Prefecture. However, the trade faltered in the face of Dutch competition, and the company decided to withdraw from Japan. In 1641, the Tokugawa Shogunate confined foreign trade to Nagasaki and granted sole rights of residence to the Dutch and Chinese.

The English East India Company factory in Hirado had mostly faded from the collective memory—and Japan was lounging in a state of peaceful seclusion—in the autumn of 1808 when HMS *Phaeton* entered Nagasaki Harbor disguised as a Dutch trading vessel. Dutch representatives rowed out to welcome the ship, but the crew took them hostage and demanded food, water and fuel. Nagasaki Magistrate Matsudaira Zushonokami Yasuhira had little choice but to bend to the British demands. The *Phaeton* sailed away two days later, but Matsudaira committed ritual suicide to take responsibility for the calamity, and the Tokugawa Shogunate, alerted to the British threat in East Asia, responded by reinforcing coastal defenses and ordering the Nagasaki interpreters to study English and to compile Japanese-English dictionaries. China's humiliating defeat in the 1839-42 Opium War only heightened the sense of alarm over British designs in East Asia.

The next important encounter between Britain and Japan occurred on September 7, 1854, when four warships of the Royal Navy anchored in the middle roadstead of Nagasaki Harbor. Admiral James Stirling met with Japanese representatives and submitted a letter requesting cooperation in Britain's struggle to block Russian incursions in the northern reaches of the Japanese archipelago. On October 14, after a six-week wait for a response

1

from the Tokugawa Shogunate, Stirling sat down with the Nagasaki Magistrate to sign the Japan-Britain Treaty of Amity.

Like the American and Russian pacts concluded a few months earlier, the treaty was purely diplomatic: Japan agreed to allow British ships to visit a few designated ports but made no concessions regarding commercial or residential rights. A period of rumination and procrastination continued until August 3, 1858 when Sir James Bruce, 8th Earl of Elgin and 12th Earl of Kincardine, arrived in Nagasaki to put the seal on a treaty that would guarantee commercial and residential privileges. One of the ships in his convoy was the *Emperor*, a sleek steam-powered yacht built on the Thames as a gift from Queen Victoria to the Japanese emperor.

Lord Elgin had expected to sign the new Anglo-Japanese treaty in Nagasaki, but he decided to accompany the *Emperor* to Edo and to deal directly with representatives of the Tokugawa Shogunate. He signed the Anglo-Japanese Treaty of Amity and Commerce, one of the epoch-making Ansei Five-Power Treaties, in Edo on August 26, 1858 and turned the yacht over to Japanese authorities the same day.

Now the stage was set for the inauguration of the Japan Consular Service, the dispatch of diplomats, and the establishment of the first British consular stations to oversee the new era of trade and communication.

Nagasaki Harbor in the Edo Period, with the fan-shaped island of Dejima in the foreground. Nineteenth-century lithograph. (Private collection)

1 JAPAN'S FIRST BRITISH CONSULATE

THE ANSEI FIVE-POWER TREATIES brought an end to five years of negotiations between Japanese authorities and representatives of the United States, Britain, Russia, France and the Netherlands. Effective July 1, 1859, they called on the Tokugawa Shogunate to open several ports including Nagasaki as sites for foreign settlements and to grant rights of free trade and extraterritoriality (exemption from local laws) to all people arriving from the five countries. Like their antecedents in China, the treaties were inherently unequal, that is, they gave advantages to one cosignatory that were not enjoyed by the other.

Scottish merchant-adventurer Kenneth R. Mackenzie arrived in Nagasaki in early 1859 to open a branch of Jardine, Matheson & Co., the powerful British *hong* that had blackened its hands in the Opium Wars and risen to prominence in the business communities of nineteenth-century China. He chose Nagasaki as a matter of course, not only because it was the nearest port to Shanghai, but also because it was still the only place in Japan with an infrastructure geared to trade and a population accustomed to dealing with foreigners.

Mackenzie found the port abuzz with activity. In addition to the residents of the Dutch factory at Dejima and the crews of a number of American and French warships visiting the port, a team of Dutch engineers was supervising an iron foundry and engine works on the other side of the harbor, Russian naval personnel had established a depot and barracks nearby, and freelancers were arriving in increasing numbers to catch a glimpse of the previously secluded country and to establish contacts with Japanese merchants and officials. For the Japanese hosts, the sudden inundation brought unexpected economic prosperity but challenged the system of trade and cultural coexistence entrenched in Nagasaki for more than two hundred years.

Fig.1-1 Taken in October 1860, Pierre Rossier's photograph of the proposed site of the Nagasaki Foreign Settlement was one of the first panoramic portraits taken in Japan. The huts of Tomachi Ōura village cluster in the foreground, with the mud flats at the mouth of Oura Creek beyond. Myōgyōji, with its flagpole flying the Union Jack, is visible on the opposite hillside. Three years after this photograph was taken, Thomas Glover built his famous house at the base of the huge pine tree on the crest of the hill. (National Archives, Kew, FO 46/8)

The village of Tomachi Ōura, formerly part of the Ōmura domain, was the proposed site of the Nagasaki Foreign Settlement, chosen beforehand by the Tokugawa Shogunate pending approval by the foreign consuls. Bordering the city to the south, the village included a coastal area with a few fishermen's huts huddling near the harbor and hillsides cut into step-like ledges for the cultivation of fruits and vegetables. The latter rose away from a creek penetrating the brim of flat land at the water's edge. The farmhouse rented by Mackenzie nestled on the hillside to the south of the creek near a Buddhist temple called Myōgyōji.

Arrival of the First British Delegation

On June 4, 1859, HMS *Sampson* sailed into the long inlet of Nagasaki carrying Rutherford Alcock, a former army surgeon appointed consul-general to Japan and leader of the first British delegation to Edo (Tokyo). The other passengers included Abel A.J. Gower, a former assistant under Alcock in the Canton (Guangzhou) Consulate, and Captain Howard Vyse and C.

4

Pemberton Hodgson, consuls-designate for Kanagawa (Yokohama) and Hakodate, respectively. George S. Morrison, the consul-designate for Nagasaki, had been delayed and unable to join the group. The men were the first members of the Japan Consular Service, organized by the British Foreign Office on the same model as the body established earlier in China.

Soon after reaching Nagasaki, Alcock arranged to rent Myōgyōji as a temporary residence for the British consular representatives, probably with the assistance of Kenneth R. Mackenzie whose rented farmhouse was located only a few steps away. Founded in 1658, the temple consisted of a large *hondō* (main hall) and a number of smaller buildings perched on the hillside overlooking Ōura Creek and the village of Tomachi Ōura. Although little more than a country temple serving the local farming and fishing community, Myōgyōji's location in the center of the proposed foreign settlement pulled it unexpectedly into a new era of contact with foreigners.[1]

While still aboard the HMS *Sampson* in Nagasaki Harbor, Alcock informed C. Pemberton Hodgson in writing of his appointment to the position of acting consul in Nagasaki:

> Finding on my arrival here that British trade to a large extent was already established and that many British firms had opened houses of business and taken up their residence at Nagasaki, I have deemed it desirable to establish a consulate at this port without delay. Mr Morrison, the consul appointed to this port, cannot be expected to arrive before the middle or end of July— prior to which the provisions of Lord Elgin signed in August last will come into effect, opening the three ports on this coast to British trade under the regulations of trade thereby annexed, probably leading to a large and rapid development of the commerce. At Hokodadi [sic] on the contrary I have no information that there is any trade under the British flag or a single British resident there. Under these circumstances I have no hesitation in appointing you provisionally—and in accordance with your wishes—to take charge of the consulate at Nagasaki.[2]

Educated at Eton and Cambridge, C. Pemberton Hodgson had traveled the world, published books about his adventures in Australia and served as British consul at Caen, France. He had been appointed along with George S. Morrison to the Japan Consular Service in a royal declaration dated February 21, 1859.[3]

---

[1] Myōgyōji remained like an oasis of Japanese culture while the foreign settlement developed around it. The buildings rented by the British no longer exist, but the temple still functions on the original site to this day.

[2] Rutherford Alcock to C. Pemberton Hodgson, June 13, 1859 (FO 262/7).

[3] *The London Gazette*, February 25, 1859.

Hodgson made an adventurous first excursion into the streets of Nagasaki while the British warship lay at anchor, only to run into a crowd of gawkers and flee back to the safety of the ship. The principal object of curiosity was apparently Mrs. Hodgson and her daughter, the first Caucasian women to set foot in Japan since the controversial stopover of Titia, the wife of Dutch Factor Jan Cock Blomhoff, at Dejima in 1817. Hodgson later reported that a Japanese artist ran along beside her, sketching away, and produced an illustration that was later converted into a woodblock print and mass-produced on a saké label but looked "as much like the original as a butterfly to a salamander."[4]

Mrs. Hodgson meanwhile wrote to her mother in England, recounting in colorful detail the startling visit ashore and other exotic sights and sounds of Nagasaki. She also provides the following description of Myōgyōji, site of Japan's first British consulate:

> Its situation is far from beautiful, being on the edge of a low cape, far from the town (which rejoiced me, as I shall see less of the people), surrounded by handsome pines, and having a limited view of the bay. We had in all seven rooms, about eight feet high, and the largest (which is small) is to be office and dining room; but a very gloomy one, I fear. My own room, which is to be 'à ma volonté,' either of one or two pieces, as I move the sliding partitions, was light and gay, with an agreeable aspect to the north and the bay. This is to be my bedroom, and every afternoon the drawing-room, for we have the society of two charming young men, who are attached to the Consulate, and are to live with us.
>
> On the whole my impression was that I would like the place. The priest and his wife were very civil, and tried all in their power to assist us, and as long as the 'Sampson' was in sight, I felt I should not be an exile here. There is to be a room for my maid and [daughter] Eva, and one room apiece for Dr. Myburgh and Mr. Annesley, and then a second office, and a large room, capacious but not clean, which is to be larder, kitchen, and dormitory for the servants.
>
> While the diplomatists were discussing graver matters, I, with the officers of the 'Sampson,' and some marines kindly lent us, and my own servants, were hastily arranging our rustic furniture in this 'maisonette Japonaise;' and with such success, that on Monday the 13th, nine days after our arrival, we were able to sleep on shore. On that same day the British flag in Japan was hoisted by my husband, with three cheers from our loyal community.[5]

---

[4] C. Pemberton Hodgson, *A Residence at Nagasaki and Hakodate in 1859-1860* (London: Richard Bentley, 1861), p 30.

[5] Ibid., p.111. The date June 13, 1859 corresponds to May 13 on the Japanese (lunar) calendar.

Mrs. Hodgson's report indicates that the inauguration of the consulate coincided with Rutherford Alcock's letter of appointment dated June 13 and therefore that the consul-general was still in Nagasaki at the time. Most descriptions of the 1859 voyage of HMS *Sampson* mention briefly that the ship stopped in Nagasaki but gloss over the fact that the first consulate was established there. The omission reflects a tendency among historians to neglect Nagasaki's role in early British-Japanese relations in favor of discussions related to Tokyo, Yokohama and Kobe. The absence of any commemorative signboard or plaque outside the temple today underlines the paucity of attention even in Nagasaki, but the fact is that the modern history of diplomatic relations between Britain and Japan began at Myōgyōji, not Tōzenji where the first British Legation was established after Alcock's arrival in Edo on June 26.

Fig.1-2 Myōgyōji, site of the first British consulate in Japan, with the town of Nagasaki in the background. Attributed to Abel A.J. Gower circa 1865. (Private Collection)

The two charming young men mentioned by Mrs. Hodgson were Francis G. Myburgh and Adolphus A. Annesley, recruited in London to serve as assistant and interpreter at the Nagasaki consulate. Myburgh was a medical doctor, while Annesley was a former midshipman in the Royal Navy whose father had served as British consul at Amsterdam. Both men had been welcomed into the Japan Consular Service because of their fluency in Dutch, the *lingua franca* of Japanese-European exchange in Nagasaki for more than two centuries and still the principal means of communication with local officials.

Despite the assistance of interpreters, Hodgson may have had trouble even writing documents and eating meals in a dignified manner. The first dispatch from the Nagasaki British Consulate—that is, the first dispatch from a British diplomatic station in Japan—was a rather urgent request, dated only two days after the opening of the consulate, for permission to purchase "a few chairs, two tables, and a large cupboard in which to deposit the consular papers and books."[6]

On July 7, C. Pemberton Hodgson penned a report on the state of affairs in Nagasaki and sent it directly to the Foreign Office in London, apologizing for not posting it through the consul-general but expressing the hope that "it will give you satisfaction to know of our progress."[7] He states that he engaged in lengthy interviews with the Nagasaki Magistrate and reached tentative decisions regarding the proposed site of the foreign settlement and the currency to be used in commercial exchanges.

The latter issue was apparently the most vexing. The Japanese government had acquiesced to an exchange rate of about three *ichibu* silver coins per Mexican silver dollar,[8] but stocks of the Japanese coin had quickly disappeared in the days following the opening of the ports, and Japanese merchants were still refusing to accept the foreign money. With prodding from Hodgson, the officials agreed to change dollars into *ichibu* when necessary and to enforce the accepted exchange rate among the mercantile community. The British consul goes on to describe his other accomplishments:

> I have selected a site for the consulate and a burial ground for foreigners, have obtained the use of a prison, established the right to hire [Japanese] servants, obtained a depot for H.M. Naval Service, fixed upon the Port Regulations and opposed the prohibition of fishing and shooting unless as a means of obtaining a livelihood. I also refused to take under British protection the swarms of Chinese who claimed it, unless such Chinese were registered at the consulate as in the service of British subjects... I propose in a few days sending your Lordship a list of all articles capable of being exported, or which, if encouraged, might be exported.

The "site for the consulate" was of course Myōgyōji, and the prison to which Hodgson alludes was part of the Japanese detainment facility in Sakura-machi, an arrangement necessitated by the lack of a lockup in the old wooden temple and the increase in delinquent behavior among British sailors.

In connection with the latter, Hodgson hired a constable to maintain law

---

[6] C. Pemberton Hodgson to Rutherford Alcock, June 15, 1859 (FO 262/7).
[7] C. Pemberton Hodgson to the Foreign Office, July 7, 1859 (FO 46/5).
[8] The relatively pure Mexican silver dollar was the common currency used by foreigners in East Asia. In Japan, it was traded weight-for-weight with the *ichibugin*.

and order and to arrest wrongdoers, a consular position that would retain its importance until the abrogation of extraterritoriality in 1899. The consul and assistants were enlisted in London on the basis of academic credentials, linguistic ability and diplomatic experience, but the constable was usually a discharged soldier or policeman from the municipal force in one of the Chinese ports engaged on the spot in Japan and paid a workingman's salary. The first constable in Nagasaki was Edward T. Kettle, enlisted from the police force in Shanghai, followed from the summer of 1860 by Matthew Green, a native of Cheshire, England and former sailor who would go on to contribute to the development of the foreign settlement.[9]

The early consular staff also included two Japanese linguists (interpreter and transcriber), two messengers, two watchmen and four boatmen.[10] Hodgson procured another small temple called Nisshinji, located above Myōgyōji, as a residence for Francis G. Myburgh, evidence that the buildings at the latter temple were too cramped for the entire delegation.

Hodgson remained optimistic about the future of the port and the potential for trade. In a subsequent letter to Rutherford Alcock, he reported that, "The exports from Nagasaki are considerable, and will probably before long be enormous, for many of the articles are quite essential to our Chinese neighbors, and others are greedily desired in Europe."[11]

Moreover, despite the opening of Yokohama and Hakodate, Nagasaki continued to serve as the gateway to Japan for most of the foreign ships sailing from China and the principal business and communication venue. Hakodate was proving impracticable because of its great distance from the centers of power, and Yokohama was still a fledgling port with little experience in foreign trade. In his book *A Diplomat in Japan*, Ernest Satow describes conditions during the early years after the opening of Japan's ports and comments on the difference between Nagasaki and Yokohama as follows:

At Nagasaki most of the territorial nobles of Western Japan had establishments whither they sent for sale the rice and other produce received in payment of tribute from the peasants, and their retainers came into frequent contact with foreigners, whose houses they visited for the purchase of arms, gunpowder and steamers. Some sort of friendly feeling thus sprang up, which was increased by the American missionaries who gave instruction in English to younger members of this class, and imparted to them liberal ideas which had no small influence on the subsequent course of events. At

---

[9] Taniguchi Ryohei, *Mrs. Mary Elizabeth Green* (unpublished Japanese manuscript, May 2010).

[10] M. Paske-Smith, *Western Barbarians in Japan and Formosa in Tokugawa Days, 1603-1868* (Kobe: J.L. Thompson and Co., 1927), pp 233-4.

[11] C. Pemberton Hodgson, p 26.

Yokohama, however, the foreign merchants had chiefly to do with a class of adventurers, destitute of capital and ignorant of commerce. Broken contracts and fraud were by no means uncommon.[12]

George S. Morrison arrived in Nagasaki on August 6—two months late—and took over from C. Pemberton Hodgson. The latter proceeded to Hakodate to open a consulate in that port, but illness forced him into retirement only two years later, and he died in France in 1865 after publishing his groundbreaking work on the first British consulates in Japan.[13]

Fig.1-3 George S. Morrison, from an insert in *The Illustrated London News*

MR. GEORGE STAUNTON MORRISON, HER MAJESTY'S CONSUL AT NAGASAKI, JAPAN.

Mr. Morrison's Tribulations

Born in Macao in 1830, George Staunton Morrison was the son of Robert Morrison, the first Protestant missionary to China and celebrated translator of the Bible into Chinese. His parents undoubtedly named him after the English traveler and scholar Sir George Staunton, Robert Morrison's forerunner in Chinese studies. The younger Morrison underwent schooling in England and entered the public service in 1848, going on to serve in various posts in China. In 1856, he was appointed First Assistant and Keeper of the Records in the Superintendency and, the following year, Secretary to the Hong Kong Government.

Not all had gone well in China. Morrison had fallen ill along with several other British residents after eating bread poisoned by a malevolent Chinese

---

[12] Ernest Satow, *A Diplomat in Japan* (Oxford University Press, 1921), p 22.

[13] Kuwata Masaru, *Kindai ni okeru chūnichi eikokugaikōkan* (British Diplomats in Japan, 1859-1945), (Kobe: Mirume Shobo, 2003), pp 307-8.

baker, and, on another occasion, he had almost been killed by shots fired from a rebel junk anchored in the harbor. He returned to Britain on leave in 1858, only a few months before his appointment as Senior Consul in Japan, a position of responsibility that would entail acting as chargé de affairs in the event of the death or absence of Rutherford Alcock.[14]

George S. Morrison was already complaining about poor health in early 1859 when, writing to the Foreign Office from the Oriental Hotel in London, he declined to take the route to China proposed by his superiors and asked for permission to board a vessel sailing directly from Liverpool to Shanghai later in the year.[15] Also, unlike his predecessor, he traveled alone, unable to enjoy the therapeutic effects of family companionship.

Upon arrival in Nagasaki, Morrison reeled in shock to see the state of his new workplace. In contrast to Mrs. Hodgson and her husband, who wrote in a rather lighthearted tone about their life and work in Nagasaki, the new consul threw his arms up in horror and astonishment, groaning in his first letter from Nagasaki that:

> The disagreement of my position exceeds all belief or power of description. We are domiciled in the outhouses and sheds of a temple which were resigned to snakes and centipedes before being appropriated for Her Majesty's consulate. The floor is of planking raised two or three feet from the ground—the ceiling of planking two or three feet above our heads. The sides of the house are of paper windows sliding in grooves, and to admit light and air they are taken out. Hence you are exposed on every side to the entrance of any thief who takes a fancy to your property, and some of the sheds occupied by foreigners have already been gutted. You make take a slight precaution by closing the plank shutters, and at the same time place yourself in complete darkness without air... This and mosquitoes swarm about your face like you were a piece of butcher's meat. Everything you possess, that the thieves leave, is destroyed by rust and mold... But I have said enough to show that our condition is <u>miserable</u> (the only word that proximally describes it).[16]

Despite several years of experience in China, Morrison seemed incapable of enduring the unpleasant if temporary conditions in Nagasaki. He continued the tirade in another letter to the Foreign Office:

> The air is at all times laden with the foul odours of a thousand cesspools, while the water procurable is little better than slow poison... Whatever the

---

[14] From a biographical sketch in *The Illustrated London News*, October 26, 1861.

[15] George S. Morrison to the Foreign Office, January 19, 1859 (FO 46/5).

[16] Ibid., August 17, 1859 (FO 46/5).

motives of those who last year invented and published the fabulous accounts of this country and its people, they have done an irrevocable injustice to those whose misfortune it is to pass a proportion of their time here dependent upon their means of economising sufficient to enable an escape from their unenviable position.[17]

The disgruntled consul nevertheless picked up the reins from C. Pemberton Hodgson and resumed discussions with the Nagasaki Magistrate regarding the problems faced by British residents trying to overcome linguistic and cultural barriers and to establish commercial ties, not the least of which was the apparent reluctance of Japanese authorities to follow the stipulations of the Ansei Five-Power Treaties.

The staff of the Nagasaki British Consulate celebrated their first Christmas and New Year in Japan and congratulated themselves on the progress made in diplomatic relations, but the spirit of the holiday was dashed a few days later when a mob of Chinese residents attacked Edward T. Kettle and sent a shockwave through the tiny British community.

Kettle arrested a Chinese ruffian for throwing a stone at him. But when he tried to march the man off to a Japanese police box at the edge of the (still proposed) foreign settlement, a horde of the man's compatriots poured out of the Chinese Quarter waving clubs and demanding his release. Other British residents arrived in time to fire guns and scare off the crowd. Kettle escaped in a boat and fled to Myōgyōji, where he informed George S. Morrison of the skirmish. Fearing further attacks, Morrison hurried to the HMS *Roebuck*, a British warship visiting Nagasaki at the time, and asked the commander to land an armed party. That was done, but the mob had already dispersed, and Morrison's subsequent supplications to the Nagasaki Magistrate failed to elicit any firm promise to arrest the perpetrators or to take preventive measures. Without commenting on the cause of the conflict or guessing the reasons for the grievances harbored by the Chinese community, the consul ends his report as follows:

The Roebuck will probably be in the neighborhood only for a few days, and but little of that time in port, while it is hopeless to look to the Japanese for assistance in an emergency. Few in number and scattered, [British residents] must still depend entirely upon ourselves until circumstances permit of the continued presence of a ship of war, the want of which is every day made more apparent.[18]

The anxiety persisted as George S. Morrison continued his negotiations with Nagasaki officials. Two issues were of particular importance: 1) the

---

[17] Ibid., September 7, 1859 (FO 46/5).
[18] George S. Morrison to Rutherford Alcock, January 11, 1860 (FO 262/18).

identification of viable merchandise and mutual agreement concerning the rules of trade, including the rate of exchange between the Mexican silver dollar and Japanese *ichibu* silver coin, and 2) the reclamation of land from the harbor, allotment of properties and other preparations for the establishment and operation of the foreign settlement. Since the Nagasaki Magistrate's Office served merely as a reception desk for the Tokugawa Shogunate, the negotiations were repeatedly stalled, sometimes for weeks on end, by the long waits for final decisions from Edo.

With regard to trade, Morrison grumbled in a report to Rutherford Alcock about the various obstacles encountered by British merchants trying to drive a wedge into the foreign trade monopolized for more than two centuries by the Dutch and Chinese. Many Japanese merchants continued to snub the Mexican silver dollar and to pass transactions through government channels, causing intolerable delays. It was difficult to hold Japanese merchants to their promises, he said, or to appeal for official intervention when contracts were breached. Morrison pointed out that Chinese merchants had no official treaty with Japan but continued to enjoy unfair privileges based on longstanding cultural and historical ties with their Japanese hosts. To make things worse, the lack of suitable storage facilities in the temporary buildings acquired in the Japanese town left merchandise vulnerable to theft and fire. Still, the British Consul ended his report on an unusually magnanimous and optimistic note: "All these obstacles to trade are such as were to be naturally anticipated; it would indeed be remarkable if they did not exist, in a country so jealous and exclusive as Japan, opened for the first time to an order of things diametrically opposed to the policy and habits of the nation; they cannot be overthrown in an instant but must be left to the operation of time and persevering endeavours gradually to overcome."[19]

Morrison informed Alcock that the trade in 1859, the year that Japan threw its doors open and embarked on a new era of international exchange, was confined largely to exports and that most of the British ships arriving in Nagasaki carried only ballast. He also submitted a summarized table that sheds a valuable light on the status of exports from Nagasaki to Shanghai during the first half of the year.[20] The table presents thirty-four export commodities including, in order of value: seaweed ($307,805), ginseng ($128,611), raw silk ($109,926), isinglass ($38,775), silk piece goods ($36,000), vegetable wax ($34,190), coal ($25,000), vegetable oil ($23,930), sea cucumber ($18,860) and dried fish ($18,680). Copper, the mainstay of Dutch exports during the Edo Period, barely made the list at $125. Coal was still being collected by primitive methods but would gain great importance a decade

---

[19] "Report on British Trade at Nagasaki for 1859" (FO 262/18/32-5).
[20] "Port Of Nagasaki: Exports During Half Year to 30th June 1859" (FO 262/18/70).

later when Scottish entrepreneur Thomas B. Glover introduced modern mining equipment at Takashima. Tea, meanwhile, although not even cited by Morrison, would shoot to the top of the export roster in two or three years when Glover, William J. Alt and other merchants established tea-firing plants in the rear quarter of the foreign settlement.

Glover and Alt, twenty-two and twenty years old respectively in 1860, moved quickly to the forefront of trade in Nagasaki and provided invaluable advice and assistance to George S. Morrison. A native of Aberdeenshire, Glover had arrived in Nagasaki in September 1859 to assist Kenneth R. Mackenzie in the local branch of Jardine, Matheson & Co. and in 1862 would establish Glover & Co., going on to serve as a prime contributor to Japanese modernization. Alt, meanwhile, had left his native London at the young age of twelve to pursue a life at sea but had taken leave of his ship in Shanghai and, after a short career in the Chinese Maritime Customs Service, had traveled to Nagasaki in late 1859 and founded Alt & Co., achieving stunning successes in the early foreign trade.

George S. Morrison pressed the Nagasaki Magistrate for cooperation in meeting treaty obligations regarding the physical and legal establishment of the foreign settlement and the smooth initiation of socio-commercial functions. The latter arranged for teams of laborers to carry gravel, build stone embankments, and install all the necessary roads, bridges, gutters and foundation walls in the new commercial district around the mouth of Ōura Creek. As to the method of renting land in the foreign settlement, Morrison suggested a down payment for each lot plus a small stipend payable yearly to the Tokugawa Shogunate as a guarantee against buildings and warehouses erected by the renter. However, the Nagasaki Magistrate overruled the proposal, insisting that each renter should pay a fixed annual fee regardless of buildings.

In May 1860, Morrison agreed tentatively that foreigners would pay an annual rental fee of $37, $28 and $12 per 100 *tsubo* (about 330 square meters) for lots on the waterfront, rear quarter and hillside, respectively.[21] The leases would be considered perpetual, that is, the renter would hold a permanent title deed and enjoy full rights of ownership to buildings but would not actually possess the land upon which the buildings stood. A renter could transfer a lease to another foreign resident with consular approval. If a renter relinquished his/her claim to a lot, ownership would revert to the Japanese government without refund. The perpetual lease was an arrangement unique to the foreign settlements of Japan that would remain in place until being unilaterally abolished by the Japanese government during World War Two.

The same month, George S. Morrison compiled a list of twenty-three regulations to be followed by British subjects—and by extension other

---

[21] "In the Matter of the Foreign Location" (FO 262/18/141-2).

foreigners—regarding entry and anchorage in Nagasaki Harbor, the conduct of seamen on shore leave and manner of dealing with violations of local laws, as well as prohibitions on the discharge of firearms, excursions beyond the limits of the *tenryō* and "riding quickly through the streets of the town." The list also stated that:

> No British Subject may establish either a boarding house, eating house, or other public house of entertainment without the sanction of the Consul and under such conditions as he may require. Any person harboring a seaman who is a deserter or who cannot produce his discharge, with written sanction from the Consul to reside on shore, will be liable to the penalty attending breach of these Regulations [not exceeding five hundred dollars, or three months' imprisonment.[22]

Approved by the British Legation in June and published for the information of the public the following year, the regulations established foundations for life and business in the foreign settlements of Japan.

George S. Morrison escaped briefly from the discomforts of Nagasaki in June 1860, leaving the consular duties to Francis G. Myburgh. The latter kept a short diary that sheds light on the activities of the consulate a year after its inauguration. It also reveals that the consul spent a considerable portion of his time in the consular court dealing with theft and other petty crimes, quarrels over business transactions, and the rowdy conduct of British sailors in the town.[23] In an entry dated June 12, he mentions a complaint from Japanese authorities about an attack on a woman in a Nagasaki teahouse (i.e. brothel) by a British sailor. Two days later, he reports that:

> I had sent for the woman who was stabbed by the sailor in the Tea-house to take her deposition. She came as far as the Custom House, when she was obliged to be taken back, owing to the painful condition of the wound. Her son, named Tahe, stated that her name was Sono, and her age 57 years. That on Sunday last the 10th instant, the Defendant, Ammat Alie, was with four other sailors in the Tea-House called Hikitaia, and while upstairs made such noise that the Plaintiff, who is mistress of the house, went up to ascertain the cause of it, when the Defendant drew his knife and cut her in the left forearm, and also damaged the screens in the room. Ordered them to appear at this Consulate on Tuesday, the 19th instant, at 11 o'clock.

Hikitaya is the former name of Kagetsu, a posh Japanese restaurant that remains in operation to this day with its buildings and gardens intact. A slash

---

[22] "Regulations for British Subjects in the Port and Harbor of Nagasaki," published in *The Nagasaki Shipping List and Advertiser*, August 14, 1861.
[23] Paske-Smith, Appendix No.15, pp 386-408.

on a wooden pillar in one of the second-floor rooms has been attributed to samurai hero Sakamoto Ryōma, but it is more likely a remnant of the disturbance caused by British sailors in June 1860.

Myburgh learned from an interpreter that the woman had not recuperated enough to make the trip to Myōgyōji. Finally on June 28, he dismissed the case because of the woman's failure to appear at the consulate, bringing the affair to a rather surprising conclusion. Whether or not the British provided further assistance to the woman or compensation for the damages to the building is unknown.

George S. Morrison was back in Nagasaki in September 1860 to follow up his list of regulations concerning the conduct of foreigners with a set of rules pertaining to the rental of lots in the Nagasaki Foreign Settlement.[24] A month later he joined John G. Walsh (U.S.A.), Joseph H. Evans (Portugal), and Kenneth R. Mackenzie (France) in drawing up the first list of lot renters in the Nagasaki Foreign Settlement. Morrison was the only career diplomat in the foursome: Walsh was proprietor of the American trading firm Walsh & Co., and Evans and Mackenzie were agents for the China-based Dent & Co. and Jardine, Matheson & Co., respectively. All of the men except Walsh were British. Moreover, the Dutch and Russian consuls did not apparently participate in the discussions, despite their status as fellow treaty powers. Entitled "Allotment of Land," the list of renters is provided in the form of a table, with separate columns for frontage and rearage.[25] The owners of business establishments were given priority in renting the waterfront lots, while public houses and hotels were banished to the rear quarter.

In a December 4, 1860 letter, Morrison notified Rutherford Alcock of his intention to reserve one of the hillside lots for the construction of a British consulate, pointing out that the lot was ideally situated "facing the entrance on the harbor, at the end of a spur running down from the hill, the inner slope of which looks over the town."[26] Although the allotment was still subject to negotiations with Japanese authorities, Morrison insisted that "the position is the best existing here and will be eagerly claimed by others it I am not authorized immediately to secure it."

George S. Morrison and his colleagues issued an order for all foreign residents still lingering in the Japanese town to move into the confines of the foreign settlement by April 15, 1862. The result was a rush to erect buildings on the properties where the groundwork had reached completion. One of the first inhabitants was Albert W. Hansard, who established a printing shop at No. 31 Ōura and launched Japan's first English-language newspaper *The*

---

[24] "Land Regulations for the Port of Nagasaki in Japan" (FO 262/173/153).
[25] FO 262/19/61.
[26] George S. Morrison to Rutherford Alcock, December 4, 1860 (FO 262/19).

Nagasaki Shipping List and Advertiser on June 22 the same year. In a letter to Rutherford Alcock, George S. Morrison relayed Hansard's request for the appointment of the newspaper as an official organ of the British government and added his personal recommendation to that effect.[27] The first issue of the four-page newspaper carried the following message at the top of its front page: "OFFICIAL NOTIFICATION—It is hereby notified that from and after this date, and until further orders, the 'Nagasaki Shipping List and Advertiser,' is to be considered the Official Organ of all Notifications proceeding from Her Britannic Majesty's Legation, Consulate General, and Consulates in Japan." This shows that Nagasaki was not only the cradle of foreign-language journalism in Japan but also the early capital of British diplomacy.

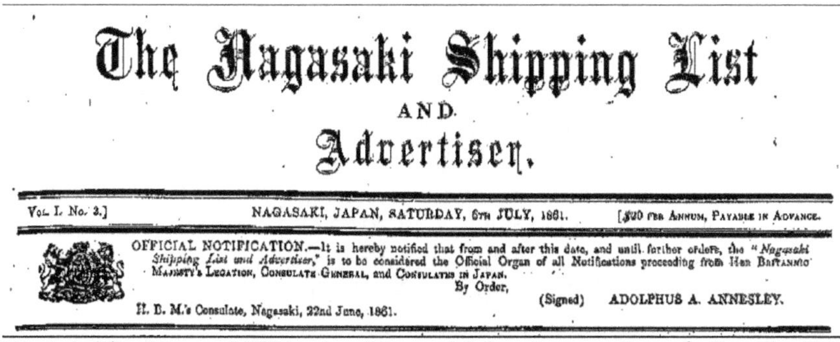

The Nagasaki Shipping List

AND

Advertiser.

Vol. I. No. 3.] NAGASAKI, JAPAN, SATURDAY, 6th JULY, 1861. [$20 per Annum, Payable in Advance.

OFFICIAL NOTIFICATION.—It is hereby notified that from and after this date, and until further orders, the "*Nagasaki Shipping List and Advertiser,*" is to be considered the Official Organ of all Notifications proceeding from Her Britannic Majesty's Legation, Consulate General, and Consulates in Japan.

By Order,

(Signed) ADOLPHUS A. ANNESLEY.

H. B. M.'s Consulate, Nagasaki, 22nd June, 1861.

Fig.1-4 *The Nagasaki Shipping List and Advertiser* was Japan's first English-language newspaper and the official organ of the British Legation.

On June 1, 1861, George S. Morrison left Nagasaki with Rutherford Alcock on the same overland journey to Edo made regularly in past decades by the Dutch *opperhooft*, passing along the old Nagasaki Road to northern Kyushu, through the Seto Inland Sea to Osaka, then down the fabled Tōkaidō Highway to the capital. Among the entourage, which assembled at Dejima and departed in a long procession through the streets of Nagasaki, was Dutch Consul-General Jan Karel de Wit, British Legation assistant Abel A.J. Gower, *London Illustrated News* artist Charles Wirgman and dozens of Japanese officials, interpreters and laborers. The month-long journey proved a great success, the travelers encountering friendliness and hospitality all along the way and enjoying sites of scenic and historic interest previously hidden from foreign eyes.

What waited for George S. Morrison and his companions in Edo, however, was not a cordial welcome but a close brush with death. On the night of 5 July, a group of angry samurai, opposed to the opening of Japan and intent on assassinating Rutherford Alcock and his staff, stormed the

[27] George S. Morrison to Rutherford Alcock, May 29, 1861 (FO 262/29).

British Legation at Tōzenji. Lawrence Oliphant, first secretary, came out of his room onto a dark corridor armed with only a hunting whip and ran into a few of the sword-wielding intruders and suffered a severe wound on his arm. Morrison, awakened by the noise, fired his revolver at the assailants and managed to defuse the immediate danger but also sustained a cut on his head during the scuffle. The intruders entered several rooms but were unable to find Rutherford Alcock. Pursued by the Japanese guards who arrived belatedly on the scene, they either fled or committed suicide by *seppuku*.[28]

The incident at Tōzenji rubbed salt into the wound of George S. Morrison's discontent in Japan. The hapless consul returned to his duties in Nagasaki but soon applied for permission to return to England to recuperate.

Morrison's Retirement

During George S. Morrison's absence, it fell on Francis G. Myburgh to oversee a number of significant business and social events in Nagasaki. He was assisted by two young businessmen, William J. Alt and Thomas B. Glover. Natives of London and Aberdeen, respectively, Alt and Glover had both arrived in Nagasaki soon after the opening of the port in 1859. The former had established the trading firm Alt & Co. and quickly erected an imposing office on the new waterfront, while the latter, starting out as an assistant to Kenneth R. Mackenzie in the Jardine, Matheson & Co. office, had joined with Francis Groom in founding Glover & Co. and had emerged as Alt's leading rival in local business and industry.

George S. Morrison may have thought when he returned to Nagasaki in April 1863 that a year and a half would have afforded ample time for improvements to living conditions in the consulate at Myōgyōji and relations between the foreign and Japanese communities. But he was disappointed on both counts.

In his first dispatch to the British Legation after returning to Nagasaki, Morrison complained that "the only persons in Nagasaki improvided [sic] with comfortable habitations are the officers of Her Majesty's Consulate, and I beg your sanction to procure for their proper accommodation on the best terms I can until such time as I am authorized to build a suitable consulate."[29]

Finally, in June, he made arrangements to move the consulate temporarily to Green's Hotel, a large Western-style building on the hillside lot directly below Myōgyōji. But, although empowered to procure new consular

---

[28] Rutherford Alcock provides a detailed account of both the overland journey and the attack on the British Legation in his book *The Capital of the Tycoon: A Narrative of a Three Years' Residence in Japan* (Harper & Brothers, Publishers, 1863) Vol. II, pp 61-158.

[29] George S. Morrison to Edward St. John Neale, 4 April 1863 (FO 262/60/7-8).

premises, Morrison had few options when it came to the *joi* (expel the foreigner) movement persisting among a small but determined samurai element throughout the country. In September 1862, during his absence, retainers of the Satsuma Domain had killed Charles L. Richardson, a British merchant from Shanghai whose horse accidentally interfered with the daimyo's procession on a narrow road in the village of Namamugi near Yokohama. The Shogunate, anxious to avoid a confrontation, had submitted a formal apology and offered an indemnity, but Satsuma officials refused to accept any responsibility, insisting that Richardson had been at fault by failing to pay proper respect to the daimyo.

Rumors circulated that Satsuma warriors and their sympathizers might at any moment launch an attack on Nagasaki as the closest foreign settlement to Kagoshima. Anxiety rose to such a level that Morrison called an emergency meeting on May 13, 1863 to decide whether or not to abandon the settlement.[30] The majority of foreign residents opted to stay and to brace themselves for a collision, stowing their valuables on ships anchored in Nagasaki Harbor and gathering for mutual protection in the Alt & Co. office on the Ōura waterfront.

For the British consul, however, the tension was intolerable. George S. Morrison wrote to his superiors in July relaying information from Thomas B. Glover that insurgents were planning an attempt on his life.[31] A few days later, he submitted a signed statement from a British physician declaring him unfit for the job of consul and recommending that he vacate his post and take up residence in Europe.[32] On July 28, 1863, Edward St. John Neale, who was acting as consul-general during Rutherford Alcock's absence, granted Morrison permission to retire from the Japan Consular Service on a pension.

Yet despite his many complaints about life in Nagasaki, Morrison had left an indelible mark on local history as the first official British consul, as a trailblazer in diplomatic negotiations, and as the architect of institutions and policies in the Nagasaki Foreign Settlement that served as precedents for those throughout Japan.[33]

British warships launched an attack on Kagoshima soon after Morrison's retirement. As a result of the skirmish, the Satsuma domain not only acquiesced to British demands but also acknowledged the importance of modernizing Japan along Western lines and promoting trade and industry. It did not mean, however, that every rightwing militant in the country gave up

---

[30] FO 262/60/28-9.
[31] "Statement of Mr. Glover, July 12, 1863" (FO 262/60/144).
[32] "Statement of William Willis M.D.," July 24, 1863 (FO 262/60/153).
[33] The 1881 UK Census (RG11/1086) shows George S. Morrison living with his wife Emma and eleven-year-old son George A. Morrison in Brighton, Sussex. He died at Nice, France on August 20, 1893. (Kuwata, p 364)

the idea of attacking foreign residents and trying to undermine the Tokugawa Shogunate's concessions to foreign powers.

Green's Hotel

From the first days after the opening of Nagasaki as a treaty port, the diplomatic representatives had been seeking a site for the construction of a permanent British consulate. One candidate was Dejima, which enjoyed proximity to the Japanese town and Chinese Quarter as well as a wide-open view of Nagasaki Harbor and cool sea breezes in summer, but the idea was foiled by the refusal of the Dutch to give up their exclusive grip on the island.

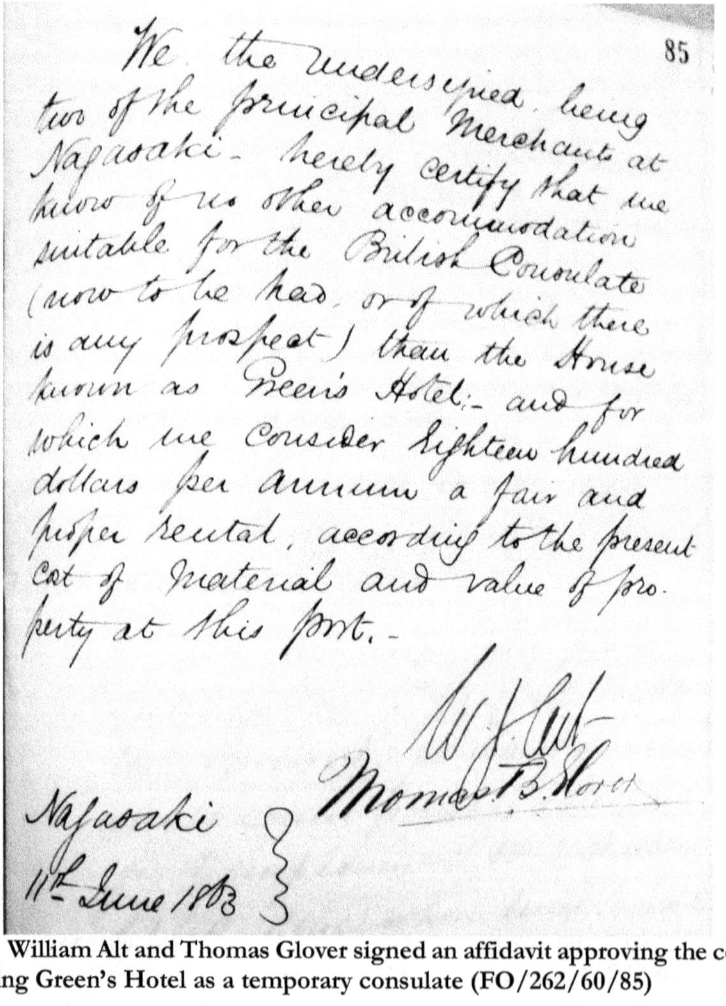
85

We the undersigned being two of the principal Merchants at Nagasaki— hereby certify that we know of no other accommodation suitable for the British Consulate (now to be had, or of which there is any prospect) than the House known as Green's Hotel;— and for which we consider Eighteen hundred dollars per annum a fair and proper rental, according to the present cost of material and value of property at this port.—

W. J. Alt

Thomas B. Glover

Nagasaki
11th June 1863

Fig.1-5 William Alt and Thomas Glover signed an affidavit approving the cost of renting Green's Hotel as a temporary consulate (FO/262/60/85)

As an alternative, George S. Morrison had obtained the perpetual lease to No. 13 Higashiyamate—the ideally situated lot he had mentioned in his December 1860 dispatch to Rutherford Alcock—and even sketched plans for the design of consular buildings, but his proposal remained on hold because of Japan's insecure political situation.

As mentioned above, Morrison arranged to move the consulate from the dingy temple to Green's Hotel in June 1863. The owner Matthew Green, who was still serving as constable, agreed to rent the facility to the British government for a period of two years at $1,800 per annum, a sizable sum that William J. Alt and Thomas B. Glover nevertheless declared "fair and proper" in a signed affidavit.[34] Considering Green's negligible salary, it is likely that he had built the hotel on the basis of a promise from British authorities to rent the building for the said period.

Green's Hotel was located at No. 11A Minamiyamate, the hillside lot directly below Myōgyōji. Constructed by Japanese carpenters in a quasi-Western style, the two-story wooden building combined chimneys and coal-burning fireplaces with a *kawara*-tiled roof and other traditional Japanese features. It stood in a bracket shape with an inner garden in the rear and a flight of stone steps leading up to the front door and verandas commanding a panoramic view over Nagasaki Harbor.

Fig.1-6 Green's Hotel was later renamed the Belle Vue Hotel and served as one of Nagasaki's most popular Western-style hotels until its closure in 1920. Picture postcard circa 1910. (Private collection)

---

[34] Green's Hotel, renamed "Belle Vue Hotel," remained in business under a succession of owners until closing in 1920. The building was later demolished. The Crowne Plaza ANA Nagasaki Gloverhill Hotel occupies the site today.

Still, the hotel was no more stable a location than the tatami-matted rooms of the old temple. After Morrison's departure, Francis G. Myburgh resumed the post of acting consul and took up the retired consul's appeals for the construction of a permanent British consulate in Nagasaki. However, the confusion and alarm lingering in the wake of the Anglo-Satsuma War sharply lowered the priority of such a project. In a letter dated September 18, 1863, Edward St. John Neale turned down Myburgh's request, pointing out that it was "impossible to enter upon the erection of new buildings when it is still so doubtful whether Nagasaki will continue to be tenable, and public affairs continue to be so uncertain and disturbed."[35]

In January the following year, Myburgh received another official letter, this time notification from Lord John Russell, Secretary of State for Foreign Affairs, of his appointment to the full position of British consul at Nagasaki as of February 1, 1864. The letter is informative because, after telling Myburgh that he was to receive a yearly salary of £1000 plus £333 for expenses, Lord Russell lays out the various obligations and restrictions related to the post of consul, undoubtedly reiterating the instructions given to every member of the Japan Consular Service similarly appointed:

> You will further understand that you are strictly prohibited from engaging directly or indirectly in trade either on your own account or on that of other persons, and that such prohibition extends to agencies of any kind or description whatever.
>
> You will be under the immediate direction and control of Her Majesty's Minister, whose instructions you will obey and to whom you will report, and to whom also you will refer in all cases of difficulty and doubt, and you will have no direct correspondence with this office.
>
> I must however strongly impress upon you the importance of acting on all occasions with prudence and moderation, of avoiding as far as possible controversy with the Japanese authorities and people, of abstaining from stopping the payment of duties and from interference in the collection of the Japanese revenue, and of so conducting yourself in all your relations both towards Her Majesty's subjects and the subjects and citizens of foreign powers as to secure not only respect for the office you hold, but the personal good will of all classes of the community among which you dwell.[36]

It was anything but easy to be prudent and moderate amid the threats of random violence that dogged the tiny foreign community of Nagasaki throughout the 1860s, when samurai from the various domains of south-western Japan frequented the port and conducted business mostly out of

---

[35] Edward St. John Neale to F.G. Myburgh, September 18, 1863 (FO 796/23).
[36] Lord Russell to F.G. Myburgh, January 20, 1864 (FO 796/26).

earshot from Shogunate authorities in Edo. Francis G. Myburgh had to deal with another serious incident soon after his appointment as consul.

On the evening of March 3, 1864, a British resident named Charles Sutton was suddenly attacked from behind by a Japanese assailant while walking home on a dark street in the foreign settlement. He suffered three potentially mortal sword wounds, including a cut below the ear apparently intended to cut off his head and two slashes that almost severed his left arm. The assassin fled when Sutton's cries attracted the attention of people nearby, precluding another probably fatal cut. Surgeons had to amputate Sutton's left arm in order to save his life.

Myburgh submitted a plea to Japanese authorities denouncing the crime and demanding that the Nagasaki Magistrate immediately apprehend the criminal. In a subsequent letter to Rutherford Alcock, he surmises as follows about the reasons for the continuing danger of violence in the foreign settlement:

> There can be no doubt that the aim of the ruffian was to take the life of a foreigner and that Sutton was not attacked because he had rendered himself obnoxious in any way to the Japanese, or because he was an Englishman. Had any other foreigner come within reach of the assassin's knife under the like circumstances, the same would have certainly befallen him… As there are supposed to be no ronings [*rōnin*, i.e. unattached samurai] in Nagasaki, it is not easy to determine who the assassin can be, whether one of the garrison of the neighboring forts returning from his day's leave and somewhat excited by liquor, or a retainer of Chosew [sic] or some other daimio hostile to foreigners. If the former, it could not then have been a premeditated attack, and I would therefore beg leave to submit that there can never be any security from such attacks until the whole of this class of retainers and minor officials, at all events during their period of residence at this port open to foreign trade, are deprived of the two swords that they now carry to no purpose… The forts and batteries also at these ports serve only as a perpetual menace against foreigners and are particularly objectionable too in being garrisoned by daimio's retainers over whom the Tycoon's [Shogun's] authorities have in reality no control, and whose hostility may be manifested at any moment.[37]

As Myburgh feared, the Japanese police failed to apprehend the criminal, even though the latter had left a shoe at the crime scene. In the aftermath, the authorities agreed to station police at the entranceways to the settlement and even offered Charles Sutton compensation in the form of a lifelong exemption from taxation. [38] But the domains of southwestern Japan

---

[37] Francis G. Myburgh to Rutherford Alcock, March 8, 1864 (FO 262/78).
[38] Sutton remained in Nagasaki and went on to succeed as a general contractor and

maintained their garrisons in Nagasaki, sword-bearing samurai were still able to stroll at liberty in the foreign settlement, and conservative views persisted among a militant element determined to embarrass the Shogunate.

Yet whatever the conflicts hampering peaceful coexistence and the development of trade and cultural exchange, William J. Alt, Thomas B. Glover and other dauntless residents—bolstered by the Japan Consular Service—continued to promote the construction of buildings in the Nagasaki Foreign Settlement and to invest in Japan's future.

Standing at the window of his office in Green's Hotel, Francis G. Myburgh enjoyed a panoramic view over the rapidly developing foreign settlement and the harbor scattered with merchantmen and warships. The reclamation of flat land and reinforcement of the waterfront along the harbor and banks of Ōura Creek had reached completion, and a large number of buildings had already appeared. The offices of trading firms like Jardine, Matheson & Co., J.C. Frazar Co. and Alt & Co. lined the Ōura waterfront, while a lower class of wooden buildings—taverns hanging out signs with names like the *Prince of Wales* and *Cosmopolite*—pressed together on the creekside and waited, beer and whisky ready, for sailors arriving in sampan-loads from ships anchored offshore.

North of the creek a cluster of shanties inhabited by Chinese laborers had sprouted up, a splinter of the old Chinese Quarter continuing from the Edo Period but still not recognized by any international treaty. Warehouses for the storage of merchandise, as well as tea-firing facilities run by Alt & Co. and Glover & Co., occupied most of the other lots behind the waterfront. The latter, housed in huge wooden sheds, consisted of rows of *kamado* fireplaces with wok-shaped pans where hundreds of Chinese and Japanese workers toiled day and night drying and packing the raw tea carried in from the hinterland. Only a few years earlier, seaweed had been the principal export item from Nagasaki to China, but now, due to the efforts of British entrepreneurs, tea had rushed to the top of the list and brought an unprecedented stimulus to the local tea-growing industry. Over the next two years, the value of exported tea would leap fourfold from $110,410 to $473,993.[39]

---

proprietor of the English-language newspaper *The Rising Sun and Nagasaki Express*. He also took over the title to No. 6 Oura, the future site of the Nagasaki British Consulate. He died of a brain hemorrhage in 1892 at the age of fifty-two and was buried at Sakamoto International Cemetery, where his gravestone can still be seen today.

[39] Sugiyama Shinya, *Meiji ishin to igirisu shōnin: tomasu gurabā no shōgai* (The Meiji Restoration and a British Merchant: The Life of Thomas B. Glover) (Tokyo: Iwanami Shoten, 1993), p 49.

Myburgh also had a clear view of the Commercial Hotel and Oriental Hotel at Nos. 25 and 26 Ōura, Western-style hostelries opened by American proprietors and furnished with Japan's earliest bars and bowling lanes. Above the hotel rooftops he could see the Higashiyamate hillside where a number of gracious colonial-style villas had appeared near the Protestant Church built in 1862 and now referred to ubiquitously as the English Church. Built in the hybrid Western-Japanese style popular in the foreign settlement, the new houses had all the features demanded by their wealthy inhabitants, such as high windows and doors, wood-strip floors ready for carpets, coal-burning fireplaces and breezy verandas.

Beyond the hillside, Myburgh saw Shinchi, an artificial island built as a site for warehouses in the Edo Period but already congested with Chinese residents moving down the hillside from the Chinese Quarter. The island of Dejima was also visible, devoid of its status as Japan's only point of contact with the Western world but still accommodating the last vestiges of Nagasaki's Dutch mercantile community.

And half-hidden by haze in the distance was the town of Nagasaki, home to some 50,000 people but quickly expanding as Japan awoke from its long slumber and joined in ever-deeper engagements with Britain and other Western powers.

Fig.1-7 The Ōura commercial district of the Nagasaki Foreign Settlement, looking north toward the old city. The large two-story building on the newly constructed Bund (waterfront street) is the office of Alt & Co. The hillside to the right is Higashiyamate. (Private collection)

2 THE YEARS IN HIGASHIYAMATE

THREE WEEKS before his departure for Yokohama in May 1864, Francis
G. Myburgh wrote to the British minister in Edo about the relocation of the
Nagasaki British Consulate, lamenting that the greater part of the five-year
existence of the consulate had been spent in temporary venues. He reports
that a local British merchant offered to finance the construction of a new
building and to lease it to the British government. He goes on to say that the
unnamed British merchant estimated that the cost would amount to about
$15,000 (Mexican silver dollars), including $900 for preparing the ground and
$600 for building fences and gates, and that he would ask for a rental fee of
25% on the outlay, or about $300 a month (exclusive of the $280 land rent
paid annually to the Japanese government). Continues Myburgh:

> These are rough estimates, but they serve to show that building is an
> expensive undertaking here—that the annual disbursements necessary for
> keeping the buildings in repair are very considerable—and that the yearly
> rent demanded is enormous. They also show that it would be far more
> economical to have the Consulate buildings erected at the public expense,
> than to have the work done by private individuals and to pay them a yearly
> rent—in five years or so the whole of the outlay will have been
> reimbursed.[40]

Abel A.J. Gower, who had been serving in the British Legation in
Yokohama, assumed the position of acting consul at Nagasaki on May 1,

---

[40] Francis G. Myburgh, Despatch No.19, April 11, 1864 (FO 796/27). Transferred
to Yokohama later the same year, Myburgh received the appointment of consul at
the newly opened port of Hyogo (Kobe) in 1867. He died of a sudden illness there
in January 1868 and was buried in the Ono Foreign Cemetery.

1864 and continued his predecessor's discussions regarding the relocation of the consulate. A native of Livorno, Italy and descendent of Sir Erasmus Gower (commander of the 1793 British expedition to the Chinese Imperial court and later governor of Newfoundland), Gower had been among the first group of British diplomatic representatives dispatched to Japan in 1859 and also among the survivors of the 1861 attack on the British Legation at Tōzenji.

Fig.2-1 Abel A.J. Gower, photographed by Pierre Rossier circa 1860.
(Yokohama Archives of History)

Although the circumstances of the move are unclear, Abel A.J. Gower states in a memorandum dated October 1, 1865 that he had relocated the consulate "during the last quarter."[41] The results of a regular Japanese survey of foreign residents conducted in the *leap month* (June-July) of 1865 corroborate that information, showing Abel A.J. Gower and the other British consular staff living at No. 9 Higashiyamate for the first time.[42] The above timeframe also fits with the contract signed in June 1863 by Matthew Green, who had agreed to rent his hotel at No. 11A Minamiyamate to the consulate

[41] A.A.J. Gower to Rutherford Alcock, October 1, 1865 (FO 796/27/39).
[42] Nagasaki Prefecture, ed., *Nagasaki kyoryūchi gaikokujin meibo* (List of Foreign Residents of the Nagasaki Foreign Settlement), (Nagasaki: Nagasaki Prefectural Library, 2004), Vol 1, p 112. During the Edo Period, *uruuzuki* (leap months) were inserted at regular intervals to correct lapses in the lunar calendar. The leap month of 1865 corresponds to early summer.

for a period of two years. The facts show that the British authorities decided not to construct a permanent consulate on the reserved lot at No. 13 Higashiyamate—probably because of the insecure political situation and Nagasaki's still uncertain future—but to follow Francis G. Myburgh's recommendation and lease an existing building.

The plot of land that would later become No. 9 Higashiyamate had been the site of a farmhouse huddling in the midst of bamboo thickets and terraced fields on the hillside overlooking Ōura Creek. Joseph H. Evans, representative of Dent & Co. and acting consul for Portugal, had rented the property soon after the opening of the port in 1859. The photograph of Higashiyamate taken by Pierre Rossier in October 1860 captures the house and the flagpole flying the Portuguese ensign beside it. When the foreign consuls divided the Higashiyamate neighborhood into lots, the site of Evans' house became No. 9 Higashiyamate. Evans left Nagasaki shortly thereafter, but the perpetual lease remained in the hands of Dent & Co., at the time one of the most powerful foreign *hongs* in East Asia.

The administrator of the property—and undoubtedly the British merchant mentioned by Francis G. Myburgh in his April 1864 dispatch—was Thomas B. Glover, representing Dent & Co. The Aberdeen native and successor to Kenneth R. Mackenzie as Jardine, Matheson & Co. agent was

Fig.2-2 Higashiyamate seen over the rooftops of the Ōura district. The British Consulate at No. 9 Higashiyamate is visible on the right with the Union Jack flying on the flagstaff. Japan's first Protestant Church (No. 11 Higashiyamate, white building on the left) was constructed to face toward the site of the martyrdom of the Twenty-Six Saints of Japan. (Private collection)

now riding a wave of success as an exporter of tea, timber, rice and other Japanese products and an importer of foreign merchandise sought by Japanese customers, everything from Indian gray shirting to iron bars and second-hand steamships. Why Glover erected the building at No. 9 Higashi-yamate remains unclear. He may have intended from the start to rent it to the British government. But it is also possible that he was following instructions from Dent & Co. to take advantage of the increased business activity in the foreign settlement and that the proposal from British authorities came later. A large two-story structure, the building featured verandas, tall shuttered windows, and a Japanese-style hipped roof with ceramic *kawara* tiles and two chimneys. It stood on a traditional *ishigaki* stone foundation with two flights of steps leading to the front entrance in an inverted V-shape that served as a backdrop for a large greenhouse. The second-story windows, framed by a series of latticed arches, commanded a panoramic view over the rooftops of the Ōura commercial district and the blue water of Nagasaki Harbor.[43]

Fig.2-3 The British Consulate at No. 9 Higashiyamate, seen from the base of Benten Bridge. The building no longer exists, but the stone foundation and inverted V-shape stairs remain to this day. (Private collection)

---

[43] The building at No. 9 Higashiyamate was demolished after sale to the Reformed Church in America in 1886, but the former Glover House remains to the present day as Japan's oldest Western-style building and a World Heritage Site.

On August 3, 1866, approximately one year after the move from Green's Hotel to No. 9 Higashiyamate, Ryle Holme of Glover & Co. wrote to the British consul expressing a wish to either sell the building "at present occupied as your consulate" for the sum of $10,000 or to sign a new lease for a period of two years at a rate of $150 a month. Holme concludes his letter with the comment that: "We are compelled to increase the rent from the present rate as entering into a lease for a time materially decreases the chance of a sale, and as you are aware we are acting for Messrs. Dent & Co. who are desirous of disposing of the property."[44] The message was forwarded to Harry Parkes (successor to Rutherford Alcock as British minister), who responded a few days later instructing the British consul to accept the terms offered by Glover & Co., with the option of extending the lease for a third year.[45] The idea of purchasing the building and establishing a permanent consulate was not aired.

In early 1866, Abel A.J. Gower moved to Hakodate to assume the position of British consul in that port, and Marcus O. Flowers, the former vice-consul at Yokohama, came to Nagasaki as his successor and moved into the consulate at No. 9 Higashiyamate with his wife Eliza.[46] A native of Buckinghamshire, Flowers had been working as an acting consul at the British consulate in Amsterdam when scouted in 1861, a time when fluency in Dutch, not Japanese, was still a prerequisite for employment in the Japan Consular Service. Now, he was destined to represent Britain during one of the most turbulent and stressful interludes in Nagasaki history.

The Meiji Restoration

The clash between conservative and progressive forces in Japan renewed fears about attacks by xenophobic elements lurking in the backstreets of Nagasaki. The nightmares of the Euro-American community came true in June 1867 when an American sailor named George Bunker died from a wound inflicted by a Japanese assailant. Then, less than two months later, two British sailors from the HMS *Icarus* met a similar violent end in the entertainment quarter of Maruyama.

The pair, Robert Foad and John Hutchings (both twenty-three years old), had landed with their shipmates expecting to enjoy shore leave in a town famous for its liberal attitudes and rowdy brothels and taverns. They proceeded to one of the establishments catering to foreigners in the

---

[44] Ryle Holme to Marcus Flowers, August 3, 1866 (FO 796/33).
[45] Harry Parkes to Marcus Flowers, August 6, 1866 (FO 796/31).
[46] Gower retired from the Japan Consular Service in 1874 and returned to his birthplace of Livorno, Italy, where he served for a time as acting British Consul. He died in 1898 at the age of sixty-two.

Maruyama district and drank themselves into such a stupor that they passed out on the street. Their friends left them to sleep it off, but when they returned they found the two men lying dead in a pool of blood. Hearing that a ship of the Tosa Clan (present-day Kōchi Prefecture) had left Nagasaki Harbor the night of the murders, Marcus O. Flowers pointed a blaming finger at the Kaientai, a group of Tosa samurai running a commercial enterprise in Nagasaki. To prove their innocence, the latter launched their own investigation and, months later, found that the crime had been perpetrated by a samurai of the Chikuzen (Fukuoka) domain and that, while ordering the guilty men to take responsibility by committing ritual suicide, the domain elders had kept the affair secret. In the meantime, the British government had concluded that the Tokugawa Shogunate was no longer able to govern its own citizens, let alone protect the life and property of foreigners. By the time the smoke cleared, the old political system had dissolved and Japan had embarked on a new era of modernization and international cooperation.[47]

Fig.2-4 Built by Thomas B. Glover for Dent and Co. and later purchased by the British government, the Western-style building at No. 9 Higashiyamate served as the Nagasaki British Consulate from 1864 to 1882. (from the Potter Album, Nagasaki University Library)

[47] FO 262/152/276-85 and 262/173/9-29).

In early 1868, the Shogunate suddenly collapsed, and Tokugawa Yoshinobu, the last Shogun, relinquished his hold on power. A band of opposition leaders proclaimed a monarchial restoration under the young Emperor Meiji and established a new government. A few days later, Marcus O. Flowers visited Nagasaki Magistrate Kawazu Izunokami to confer with him about the measures being taken to prevent chaos in the city. Kawazu replied that he had received no news or instructions from the defunct Shogunate. On the contrary, he surprised the consul by asking for British assistance in protecting his family and personal belongings. Flowers replied that any measures taken by the British, including the deployment of warships in Nagasaki Harbor, "would be for the protection of the foreign settlement only, and that Britain would preserve strict neutrality in any struggle that might take place."[48] It may be no coincidence, however, that Kawazu hastily removed his belongings from the magistrate's office and fled the city on a British ship only two nights later.[49]

In March 1868, as though sighing in relief at the resolution of domestic conflict, the British government finally decided to purchase the building at No. 9 Higashiyamate rented to date from Glover & Co.[50] Now, for the first time since the opening of Japan's doors in 1859, the Nagasaki British Consulate could fly the Union Jack over a building of its own. British authorities nevertheless showed no intention to relinquish the reserved consular lot at No. 13 Higashiyamate.

Although the sporting of swords and daggers by samurai was yet to be prohibited—and the fires of civil unrest continued to flare in some parts of Japan—the return of political stability assured most foreign residents that the threats to their personal safety had been removed and that the Japanese majority regarded international trade and the introduction of European technology and social systems as the country's best alternative. The last recorded encounter between a foreigner and an armed samurai in Nagasaki occurred in August 1868 and earned only jocular coverage in *The Nagasaki Times*, now the official organ of the Nagasaki British Consulate:

A gentleman, who had evidently not been imbibing 'the cup that cheers but not inebriates,' while wending his way homewards on Thursday last, in the 'wee sma' hours' of the morning, fell in with some yaconins [*yakunin*, i.e. samurai] having a dispute with a coolie. Being one of those large-souled

---

[48] "Memorandum of Interview between H.B.M. Consul and the Governor of Nagasaki on February 6, 1868" (FO 262/152/21-2).
[49] Nagasaki City ed., *Nagasaki shishi nenpyō* (Nagasaki City Chronology) (Nagasaki, 1981), p 104.
[50] W.G. Aston to the Chief Land Officer, Nagasaki, March 5, 1868 (*Raikan* [Official correspondence from foreign delegations to the Nagasaki Prefecture government], 1868, Nagasaki Museum of History and Culture).

individuals who always side with the weakest party, no matter how much they be in the wrong, he commenced expostulating with the samurai, who did not take much notice of him till he began to get more demonstrative in his movements, whereupon one of them drew his sword upon the adventurous foreigner, who, being well up in the sword exercise, was preparing to defend himself with his umbrella, when his friends arrived on the scene, and drew him out of the hands of the Philistines. He ought to thank his stars he escaped so easily, and doubtless it will be a lesson for him to be more careful in the future.[51]

In September the following year, Prince Alfred, Duke of Edinburgh traveled to Tokyo (the recently renamed Edo) to visit the still only seventeen-year-old Emperor Mutsuhito (Meiji) and to seal the bond of friendship between Britain and Japan. The first European royal family member to meet the emperor, Prince Alfred received an enthusiastic welcome from the people of the capital, a gesture that signaled Japan's emergence from the shadows of xenophobic isolation into the light of international exchange.[52] When the prince called at Nagasaki on his way back to China, Marcus O. Flowers and other representatives of the foreign community illuminated the entire length of the Nagasaki waterfront in welcome and accepted an invitation to an audience aboard the prince's flagship *Galatea*. Flowers later sent a letter to the governor of Nagasaki, Nomura Morihide (Sōshichi), thanking him for firing a twenty-one-gun salute as a gesture of welcome.[53]

The Christian Problem

One controversial issue carried over intact from the Edo Period—and one in which the British government took special interest—was the ban on Christianity. While granting permission for the construction of churches in the foreign settlements, the Meiji government still strictly outlawed the religion in the Japanese community. Priests of the Société des Mission Etrangères de Paris (Paris Foreign Missions Society) arrived in Nagasaki in 1863 and built a Roman Catholic church at No. 1A Minamiyamate, only a few steps from Myōgyōji and Green's Hotel, exercising the same treaty rights that had allowed the construction of Japan's first Catholic church in Yokohama and first Protestant church in the Higashiyamate neighborhood of Nagasaki in 1862.

The church was a concession granted exclusively to foreigners, but less than a month after the consecration ceremony in February 1865, a group of

---

[51] *The Nagasaki Times*, August 8, 1868.
[52] Hugh Cortazzi, "Royal Visits to Japan in the Meiji Period, 1868-1912" in *Britain and Japan: Biographical Portraits Vol.*II, Ian Nish (ed.), (Routledge, 1997), pp 79-93.
[53] Marcus O. Flowers to Nomura Soshichi, September 28, 1869 (*Raikan*, 1869).

peasants from the Urakami district appeared at the front steps and revealed their faith to one of the priests. The priests began to make clandestine visits to Urakami and other villages, conducting Mass and baptisms and re-introducing the religious tenets lost during the silence of more than two centuries. As a result, they exposed the underground Christian communities and incited the anger of Japanese authorities trying to maintain the status quo.

The Meiji government responded by banning all further sightseeing visits to the churches in Nagasaki and Yokohama, arresting native Christian leaders and threatening to exile the entire Urakami community to other parts of Japan if they refused to recant. Harry Parkes instructed Marcus O. Flowers to communicate with the governor-general of Kyushu and to convey his concern. Flowers sent two letters in May and June 1868 calling on the government to consider the international reaction and to desist from further persecutions, but he failed to influence official policy. The exodus began on July 11 with the exile of 114 Christian leaders on a steamship from Nagasaki. Their destinations were Hagi (Yamaguchi Prefecture), Tsuwano (Shimane Prefecture) and Fukuyama (Hiroshima Prefecture), where, it was hoped, they would readopt the spiritual traditions of mainstream Japan.[54]

A few days later, Marcus O. Flowers and the other foreign consuls in Nagasaki addressed the governor-general again, insisting that, "Our motives in making these enquiries are not, as we stated before, to interfere in the internal affairs of the country, but merely to point out in the most friendly way that any outrage against humanity committed against innocent persons only because they profess the Christian faith cannot but injure the reputation of the Japanese government in the eyes of the civilized world."[55]

Flowers also sent a long report to Harry Parkes, informing him of recent developments and describing a visit that he had received from Kido Junichirō (Kōin), a Chōshū samurai and politician sent to Nagasaki to handle the Christian affair. The young British interpreter and diplomat Ernest Satow was also on hand, recalling later that Kido had been accompanied to the consulate by fellow Chōshū samurai Itō Shunsuke (Hirobumi), the future prime minister of Japan.[56] Flowers ends his report with a grim assessment of the attitude prevailing in Japanese society:

> I have been informed from private sources that there is a very strong feeling among the better class of Japanese against these Christians, and the measures that the Governor has put in force are not popular. They consider that they are not half severe enough, and that the Christians ought to be

[54] Kataoka Yakichi, *Nihon Kirishitan Junkyōshi* (A History of Christian Persecutions in Japan) (Jiji Tsushinsha, 1979), pp. 624-47.
[55] The treaty consuls of Nagasaki to the Governor-General of Kyushu, July 11, 1868 (FO 262/152).
[56] Satow, p 271.

treated as criminals for breaking the laws of their country. Their animosity may arise from the fact that all of the Christians belong exclusively to the lower class. They are small farmers, farm labourers and artisans.[57]

Despite the cries of protest from foreign delegations, the remaining Christians, young and old, were rounded up in stages from January 5, 1870. The English-language newspaper *The Nagasaki Express* quickly reported on the situation, broadcasting news that would spread beyond Japan and cause outrage in Europe and the United States and exert further pressure on the Meiji government to amend its ruthless policies:

> About the same time we were issuing our copy of last week, a report was current that even then more Christians were being collected and were to be deported in the steamer *Elgin*, then at anchor off the native town of Nagasaki. Enquiries result in, a band of about 70 men having been seen that afternoon, tied in the same manner as those already made prisoners, and supposed to be Christians, being marched through the town. A certain degree of excitement, therefore, prevailed amongst those foreigners who sympathise with these unhappy people.[58]

The efforts of foreign consuls and journalists finally came to fruition in February 1873, when the Meiji government lifted the ban on Christianity and tacitly acknowledged religious freedom. By that time, a total of 3,394 people had been exiled to twenty different locations, and some 600 deaths recorded. Referred to as *yonban kuzure* (fourth collapse) in Japanese history books and remembered in the annals of Nagasaki Christians as the *tabi* (journey), the ordeal steeled the Urakami community for the hardships that followed, not the least of which would be the atomic bombing of 1945.

The surviving Christians returned to their villages and resumed their lives safe from persecution, guided by the French priests who stationed themselves in all of the former underground Christian enclaves across the prefecture. The Protestant missionaries dispatched to Nagasaki, including members of the Church Missionary Society, were also able to leave the boundaries of the foreign settlement, to build churches and seminaries in the town and to seek converts in the Japanese community.

Chinese Competition

Unlike Yokohama and other ports, Nagasaki had a Chinese community that dated back to the early seventeenth century and enjoyed longstanding commercial and cultural links with its Japanese neighbors. From the first days

---

[57] Marcus O. Flowers to Harry Parkes, July 15, 1868 (FO 262/152).
[58] *The Nagasaki Express*, February 12, 1870.

after the opening of the port, Euro-American residents begrudged the presence of Chinese squatters in the foreign settlement and the competition they posed in the arena of trade, both deemed unfair because the Qing government had not concluded a treaty with the Tokugawa Shogunate. In the autumn of 1860, little more than a year after the opening of the port, George S. Morrison wrote to Rutherford Alcock in Edo complaining as follows about the situation:

> In former times, the Chinese were subject to the same restrictions as the Dutch, but since other nations have acquired privileges the Japanese (in a spirit which must be allowed to be liberal) have admitted the Chinese to the enjoyment of the same. In fact, as my dispatches at the time showed, they bid fair at one time, taking advantage of the facilities which foreign powers had obtained to monopolize the trade and to override us with their numbers. Indeed, their demeanor in the streets was offensive and swaggering as that of only Chinese can be. The end which must have followed was foreseen and checked by the measures which I initiated in conjunction with the American Consul and which after a year's discussion and explanation the Japanese are beginning to carry out. In truth they are very shy in their dealings with the Chinese, either from fear of them as an extensive and near neighbor or from respect for them as the source of many things Japanese—in manners, customs and literature—or perhaps from a mixture of these sentiments and even of a little sympathy, for there is certainly less fundamental difference between the Japanese and Chinese than between them and Western nations.[59]

As Morrison points out, Chinese residents vastly outnumbered other foreign nationalities, despite their lack of official recognition. In 1865, among a total 397 foreigners living in Nagasaki, 246 or more than 60% were Chinese, a proportion that would persist throughout the foreign settlement period.[60] It is little wonder that the sixty-six Britons resident in Nagasaki the same year—the largest Western representation—felt some uneasiness about the Chinese presence in the city and the threat it posed to their livelihood.

Chinese residents nevertheless played an important role as interlocutors for British and American merchants and a buffer between the European and Japanese communities. Some Chinese residents established offices, shops and restaurants in the gray-zone of the Hirobaba neighborhood, while others found positions under the wing of leading foreign merchants such as John Major, William Alt and Thomas Glover. During the period from 1862 to 1870, some 1,150 Chinese were employed in foreign trading firms in Nagasaki. Thomas Glover, for one, hired 132 Chinese assistants during the

---

[59] George S. Morrison to Rutherford Alcock, October 13, 1860 (FO 262/19)
[60] Nagasaki City Chronology, p 101.

period and relied on them for help in communicating with Japanese clients and handling the export of tea and other products to China.[61]

The Meiji Restoration opened the door to a new era of prosperity and international exchange but did little to reduce tensions between the Western and Chinese communities of Nagasaki. The English-language newspaper *The Nagasaki Times*, published for about a year from April 1868, is riddled with complaints about the nuisance allegedly caused by Chinese residents, everything from garbage piled up on the streets to the sound of strange musical instruments and the din of firecrackers let off during Chinese holidays. Few European residents expressed regret or pity when a fire ripped through the Chinese Quarter in November 1869 and destroyed most of the old buildings. Acting British consul Adolphus A. Annesley weighed in on the subject in his annual report on Nagasaki affairs in 1869:

> I am glad to be able to report that the large and objectionable colony of Chinese who have been living in the settlement with no authority to control them and who have proved since the opening of this port to foreign trade a source of much trouble and have been formidable and successful competitors with the foreign merchants in their commercial transactions are now placed under the strict jurisdiction of the local authorities, and many who could give no account of themselves have been compelled to return to their country. The Chinese Guild in Nagasaki, which had existed for ages and into which foreigners were not permitted to enter, was burnt down in the past year. This fire cleared a large space of ground, the rotten and filthy houses erected thereon being been nearly all consumed.[62]

Only in late 1871, when representatives of the Japanese and Chinese governments sat down in Tientsin to sign the Sino-Japanese Friendship and Trade Treaty, did the Chinese residents of Nagasaki gain a legal foothold in the foreign settlement and welcome an officially designated diplomat to establish a consulate and assume duties commensurate with those of his British and American counterparts.

In the Consular Court

By the time the dust settled in the wake of the Meiji Restoration, the Nagasaki Foreign Settlement had grown from a roughshod outpost inhabited by "the disorderly elements of California adventurers, Portuguese desperadoes,

---

[61] Chin Tōka, "Nagasaki kyoryūchi no chūgokujin shakai" (The Chinese Community in the Nagasaki Foreign Settlement), *Nagasaki kyoryūchi gaikokujin meibo III* (List of Foreign Residents of the Nagasaki Foreign Settlement, Vol.3), (Nagasaki: Nagasaki Prefectural Library, 2004), pp 492-510.
[62] FO 262/196/134-5.

runaway sailors, piratical outlaws and the moral refuse of European nations"—as the disgusted bishop of Hong Kong had lamented in 1860[63]—into a multinational community with an increasing number of women and children.

Foreign merchants had established relationships of trust and cooperation with their Japanese counterparts, a wide variety of merchandise was exchanging hands in the port, and most of the staples and foods previously in short supply—such as milk, bread and beef—were now easily available. By 1868, the commercial districts and hillsides were replete with Western-style buildings allowing Europeans to enjoy a safe and comfortable lifestyle with all the amenities of a port town in Canada or Australia.

However, the Meiji Restoration cast a shadow on Nagasaki's time-honored role as Japan's window to the world. Many of the foreigners who had invested initially in Nagasaki concluded that Yokohama held greater potential because of its proximity to the center of Japanese power. The opening of Kobe and Osaka as treaty ports in 1868 only added to the run on Nagasaki's business fortunes. William J. Alt, one of the pillars of Nagasaki business to date, left the port in October 1868 to open a branch office in Osaka.

Foreign firms like Glover & Co. that dealt in weapons and ammunition found themselves in particularly dire straits when the return of peace pulled the plug on a lucrative source of income. Moreover, since so much of Glover & Co.'s business had been based on speculation and gentlemen's agreements with local domains, the political upheaval following the Meiji Restoration made it difficult not only to sell rifles and bullets but also to recoup debts and placate the worries of creditors like Jardine, Matheson & Co. In late 1868, Thomas Glover dissolved the partnership of Glover & Co. and revamped the company business, turning the various departments over to former employees and saving his own energy for the promotion of modern industries in collaboration with Japanese colleagues, including the Takashima Coal Mine, the Kosuge Ship Repair Dock and the Osaka Mint.

Those endeavors were successful but did not come on line soon enough to rescue Glover & Co. from financial disaster. Although willing at first to go along with Glover's reckless business activities, Jardine, Matheson & Co. decided to suspend involvement when his inability to meet obligations became obvious. In August 1870, Glover filed for bankruptcy in the British consular court.[64] One of the Scotsman's most urgent problems was an unpaid debt of some £20,000 (about $90,000) to the City of Glasgow Bank, a loan taken during the construction of a 1,500-ton corvette called the *Jho Sho Maru*, ordered from the Aberdeen shipyard of Alexander Hall & Co. for sale to the

---

[63] George Smith (Bishop of Victoria), *Ten Weeks in Japan* (London, 1861), p 263.
[64] *The Nagasaki Express*, August 27, 1870.

Higo (Kumamoto) Clan. Although a catalyst for the downfall of Glover & Co., the corvette, renamed *Ryūjo* and donated to the government, would go on to become the first warship of the new Imperial Japanese Navy and Emperor Meiji's flagship on a tour around Japan in 1872.

NOTIFICATION.

In Her Britannic Majesty's Court, at Nagasaki, Japan.

THE BANKRUPTCY ACT 1869.

In the matter of proceedings for liquidation by arrangement or composition with creditors instituted by THOMAS BLAKE GLOVER and KENNETH ROSS MACKENZIE, trading under the style and firm of GLOVER & Co.

Notice is hereby given, that a first general meeting of the creditors of the abovenamed persons has been summoned, to be held at Her Britannic Majesty's Consulate, Nagasaki, on the Sixteenth day of September 1870, at two o'clock in the afternoon precisely.

A. A. ANNESLEY,
H. B. M.'s Acting Consul.

Nagasaki, 22nd August, 1870.

Fig.2-5 The bankruptcy of Glover & Co. and related court proceedings were announced by A. A. Annesley in *The Nagasaki Express.*

Marcus O. Flowers was still on home leave, making it the responsibility of Adolphus A. Annesley, acting consul, to handle all the related work. Hearings held at the consulate over the following weeks revealed that Glover & Co. had amassed debts amounting to tens of thousands of dollars and piled up a list of creditors so long that it would take years to settle all the outstanding accounts. The Netherlands Trading Society assumed the role of liquidator and took over control of the Takashima Coal Mine and other profitable assets. Glover would remain in Nagasaki for the next six years to pay off his debts before moving to Tokyo to take up a new career as a consultant for the rapidly expanding Mitsubishi Company and foreign advisor to Japanese officialdom.

As indicated by the above, the British consul was still spending a considerable portion of his time in the consular court dealing with crimes committed by British subjects and disputes over business transactions. He could enlist assessors from the local community to act as kind of jury, and he could appeal to the minister in Tokyo for guidance in difficult cases. In 1865, the British government even tried to ease the burden by placing the consular courts under the umbrella of the Supreme Court in Shanghai. But that did not change the fact that the men working in the Japan Consular Service had scant training in legal matters. Even the chief judge at Shanghai complained that it was as if "your lordship insisted upon appointing me chief surgeon to a London hospital."[65] The dilemma deepened when the case tried in the consular courtroom involved both Japanese and British citizens, because the consul's decision was bound to be viewed as biased if it fell in favor of the foreign accuser or accused.

In February 1870, Japanese authorities notified Adolphus A. Annesley about two Britons charged with breaking into a house in the Japanese town and assaulting an elderly woman resting there. Annesley set a date for the consular court and summoned the plaintiff and defendants. A few days later, he sent a report on his verdict to the Nagasaki Commissioner of Foreign Affairs, stating that he had found the defendants guilty of illegal entry and stealing a lantern but that "it is not proven to the Court that any injury has been done to the old woman... and that it appears to the Court that she was more frightened than hurt." In the report, he declared that he had castigated the two Britons and warned them never to repeat the crime, and he added a postscript informing the commissioner that he was enclosing "herewith the sum of 9¾ boos (*ichibu* silver coins) being the amount claimed by the house owner for the damage done to his property."[66]

In another case heard by Adolphus A. Annesley, John J. Quin, the consular assistant in Nagasaki, was charged with assaulting a young Japanese man employed as a servant in his house. Quin answered the charge, reporting that he had discovered the servant in the act of theft and had tied him to a pillar and left him there for several hours. "I was aware that according to the Japanese law the crime of stealing things, which were placed in his charge, was very great," explained Quin," "and I was of opinion that for his own sake it was better to give him a slight punishment myself than to deliver him over to his own authorities whose punishment would no doubt have been much heavier." At Annesley's behest, Quin penned a formal apology, which the acting consul forwarded to the Commissioner of Foreign Affairs with his own letter. The lack of any subsequent correspondence indicates that the gesture was sufficient to bring the issue to a close.

Marcus O. Flowers returned to Nagasaki only to face an unrelenting succession of court cases in the hearing room at No. 9 Higashiyamate, everything from illegal entry and theft to neglect of duty, attacks by dogs,

---

[65] J.E. Hoare, "Britain's Japan Consular Service, 1859-1941," *Britain & Japan: Biographical Portraits Vol. II* (Ian Nish [ed.], The Japan Library, 1997), p 102.
[66] Adolphus A. Annesley to the Commissioner of Foreign Affairs, Nagasaki, February 18, 1870 (*Raikan*, 1870).

noise complaints and squabbles over the late delivery of merchandise. The burden was such that he spent as much time listening to testimony from plaintiffs and defendants as negotiating with Japanese officials, promoting British trade and fulfilling other important consular duties. To make things worse, he also had to handle court cases involving people of Swedish, Spanish and Austro-Hungarian nationality in accordance with Britain's agreement to represent those countries in Japan.

One of the most persistent headaches was the poor behavior of seamen visiting the port. On September 30, 1874, Flowers heard the case of James Collington, a British sailor on the man-of-war HMS *Iron Duke* who had been detained by the Japanese police on charges of creating a disturbance in a Nagasaki house and drawing a knife at the time of arrest. The trial log preserved in the consular archive includes statements from a Japanese maid named Yei as well as the owner of the house, Oda Jokichi, and several other servants, two policemen, and the defendant. [67] The police accused Collington of entering the Oda family house by the rear door, molesting Yei when she emerged naked from the bath, assaulting two servants who caught him in the act, seizing a knife in the kitchen and using it to scare off the servants as he made his escape, then resisting the Japanese police who pursued and arrested him in Motokago-machi, where again he allegedly pulled out the knife and wielded it in a menacing manner.

Collington stated that he had imbibed liquor at a tavern in Ōura and that he had no memory of his actions between his departure from the tavern and his arrest, but he denied the accusation of violence, saying, "As for drawing a knife, or striking the police, I did not do it." The Japanese witnesses testified unanimously that Collington had in fact seized and wielded the knife, and both of the policemen who arrested him stated that, in an act of self-defense, they had struck him on the legs with their batons and forced him onto the ground, at which point they took away the knife, handcuffed him, and conveyed him to the police station on a rickshaw. Gerard Irvine, surgeon on the HMS *Iron Duke*, told the court that Collington had suffered a broken knee in the scuffle, an injury so severe that he was "maimed for life."

After hearing all the testimony, Marcus O. Flowers delivered the following decision: "The Court considers the charge of assault and causing a disturbance proved, and fines prisoner three dollars and costs. The charge of drawing a knife, the Court considers not proved to its satisfaction." In other words, with regard to the far more serious crimes of attempted rape and intimidation with a deadly weapon, the sworn testimony of two Japanese policemen corroborated unwaveringly by several eyewitnesses was deemed less reliable, or at least no more reliable, than the claim of a drunken British sailor with a broken knee.

---

[67] FO 262/262/220-229.

As long as the foreign settlement existed as an official entity, Japanese police trying to enforce the laws of their country and foreigners insisting on their legal immunity were bound to collide. The ban on opium was one law about which Japanese authorities were particularly and understandably adamant, having seen the political, financial and moral damage that the drug had caused in China. Even British physicians and pharmacists like William Jalland ran into trouble when trying to import opium-based medicines for use in the foreign settlement. Jalland had to submit a deposition in April 1874, countersigned by Marcus O. Flowers and formalized with the Nagasaki British Consulate seal, swearing that he was importing opium for medicinal purposes only.[68] In another case, a bottle of Battley's Solution (a sedative made from opium dissolved in alcohol) imported from Shanghai by British physician William Renwick was confiscated by Nagasaki Customs, triggering a lengthy exchange of appeals and rebuttals between the British Consulate and Japanese authorities.[69]

Despite the efforts of police and customs officials, the smuggling and surreptitious use of opium persisted, not only in the shadowy back lanes of the Shinchi Chinese Quarter, but also among Chinese workers employed by European companies in the foreign settlement. In March 1875, Japanese police entered the tea-firing factory of Maltby & Co. at No.23 Ōura and arrested a Chinese employee who had been found smoking opium. John Maltby, the owner of the company, wrote a letter of protest to Marcus Flowers, insisting that the police had no right under treaty regulations to enter his property without permission. Flowers conveyed the complaint to the Governor of Nagasaki, who responded by allowing the employee to return to the factory—only to have him re-arrested and marched back to prison where he was sentenced to eighteen months hard labor in the Takashima Coal Mine. The case rested there, with no further opportunity for British intervention.[70]

The English-language newspapers of Nagasaki regularly carried reports on the cases tried in the British and American consular courts, as much for entertainment value as for importance in the daily affairs of the foreign settlement. One was a sensational case of attempted murder that sent ripples of shock through the foreign community in October 1877, exposing the ghetto of drunkenness and violence on the south bank of Ōura Creek and the back streets of the commercial district..

On October 24, 1877, Marcus O. Flowers heard the case of John J. Johnson vs John Kelly, with prominent British residents Frederick Ringer

---

[68] FO 796/61.
[69] FO 262/341/8-19.
[70] FO 262/277.

and Thomas Hellyer serving as assessors. [71] Johnson was an African-American former sailor from Baltimore, Maryland who had been living in Nagasaki since the early 1860s, operating taverns with names like Board of Trade Saloon, Pacific Hotel and Brooklyn House. The defendant, J.F. Goodwin Kelly, apparently another barkeeper in the neighborhood, was charged with firing a revolver several times in Johnson's tavern and wounding a bystander named McNabe. The erratic testimony of the various men involved—a motley collection of desperadoes who had probably landed in Nagasaki as drifters or discharged seamen—reads like the description of a gun fight in a lawless Wild West saloon. Marcus O. Flowers, seconded by Ringer and Hellyer, decided:

> that the prisoner had on the 7th instant got into bad company, and that he had been made a fool of by certain persons who had a grudge against Dougherty and Johnson; that prisoner was not sober at the time he entered Johnson's house, and that he was provoked into discharging a revolver, owing to Dougherty having in the first instance pointed and snapped a pistol at him; that the prisoner was fortunate in not having wounded Dougherty, whom the prisoner had first threatened to assault; that had he wounded Dougherty the case would have been far more serious, and that he would have been committed for trial; that he had unfortunately wounded McCabe, an unconcerned person, against whom he had no grudge; that Dougherty, Keegan, Curtis and Swinson had not stated all they knew, and that their statements were contradictory and unreliable; that it was not proved who owned the revolver; and that, taking the above extenuating circumstances into consideration, he would sentence him to six weeks imprisonment.

Although the publication of trial logs in the English-language press declined in subsequent years, the courtroom in the British Consulate continued to see a sorry procession of residents complaining about derailed business deals and trivial issues related to land claims and noise irritations, as well as sailors dragged in front of the consul to answer charges of engaging in drunken brawls, damaging property and failing to return to ship on time.

While the foreign consuls struggled to maintain law and order and bring miscreants to justice, Protestant missionaries looked down indignantly from their hillside residences at the foreign sailors running amok in bars, brothels and gambling dens. The missionaries made repeated attempts to rescue sailors from sin by opening rest homes and reading rooms in the foreign settlement, but the problem of prostitution, the sleazy netherworld of taverns in the foreign settlement, and the poor behavior of sailors and vagabonds continued to bolster Nagasaki's reputation among missionaries and naval

---

[71] *The Nagasaki Express*, October 27, 1877.

authorities as a "second Corinth." [72]

The following comment, published in the English-language press, indicates the stubborn persistence of the controversy and the social tensions dividing the well-to-do and not-so-well-to-do segments of the foreign community:

> The Sagarimatsu side of the Oura Creek, the buildings on which, from the Customs House to the native town, with one solitary exception, consist of grog-shops from one end to the other, has for years past been a standing disgrace to the otherwise peaceful and respectful foreign settlement of Nagasaki; and as time rolls on matters in that particular quarter are by no means improving… There are undoubtedly a few—a very few—[barkeepers] who for a long time have conducted themselves in such a manner that, all things considered, not a word can be said against them, and their reputation for peace-abiding citizens is thoroughly established. But, on the other hand, it is equally undeniable that there are amongst them quite a number who, under proper government, would long ere this have been forced into reformation or relegated to life service in a chain-gang, most probably the latter! Drinking, fighting, and every other description of debauchery, day and night, seem to be the height of their ambition, and the only thing they live for. Breaking one another's heads with bottles and clubs, thus disfiguring each other for life, seems to be looked upon as a gentle pastime; and if the present mild way of treating such offences is continued they will soon become of daily occurrence. So far as this class of pariahs themselves are concerned, it might perhaps be almost as well to let them follow the reported example of certain cats of Kilkenny, who fought until nothing remained of them but their toe-nails and a tuft of hair; but the process would be a very long one and very demoralising to others while it lasted.[73]

Whether it was the confessional in the Catholic church, the Protestant mission rest home, or the shabby tavern teetering on the bank of Ōura Creek, the Nagasaki Foreign Settlement continued to serve as a cushion for the seamen bumped from one port to another on the rising tides of Euro-American involvement in East Asia in the latter half of the nineteenth century. And the judiciary duties of the British consul and the constable assigned to arrest and imprison troublemakers in the consulate jail would not end until the summer of 1899 when Japan finally achieved autonomy over legal issues within its own national borders.

---

[72] H.B. Johnson, "Nagasaki and its Missions," *The Gospel in All Lands* (1897), p 61.
[73] *The Rising Sun and Nagasaki Express*, August 31, 1887.

3 ON THE WATERFRONT

THE BRITISH GOVERNMENT maintained the lease to No. 13 Higashi-yamate even though almost a decade had passed since George S. Morrison acquired the lot for the construction of a permanent consulate. In November 1870, Aldolphus A. Annesley wrote to Harry Parkes informing him that the governor of Nagasaki had issued a title deed for the 3,092-*tsubo* (about one hectare) "reserved consular lot" and that the yearly land rent of $365.04 had been paid to date.[74] He even supplied a map of the property showing the borders with adjacent lots and the position of roads, further evidence that British authorities intended to build consular premises there. For some reason, however, the scheme remained on hold.

The failure to arrive at a decision in Nagasaki may have been due, not just to an ongoing lack of confidence in Nagasaki's future, but also to events in Shanghai and Yokohama. The consulate buildings in Shanghai burned to the ground only a few weeks after Annesley's letter, and British authorities were busy trying to remove the British Legation from the Yokohama Foreign Settlement to a more suitable site in the heart of Tokyo, circumstances that undoubtedly pushed Nagasaki back on the queue of official priorities. In 1871, the British government acquired the lease to a plot of land outside the Hanzōmon Gate of the Imperial Palace (site of the present-day British Embassy) in Tokyo and began the task of erecting buildings and transferring diplomatic functions, taking a period of four years to move the legation in its entirety from the safe zone of Yokohama to the seat of national government.[75]

One of the key figures in both the reconstruction of the consulate in Shanghai and the establishment of the British Legation in Tokyo—as well as

---

[74] Adolphus A. Annesley to Harry Parkes, November 25, 1870 (FO262/196).
[75] J.E. Hoare, *Embassies in the East*, Routledge, 1999), p. 111-5.

the design of the first consulate at Kobe—was Robert H. Boyce, an architect employed as a surveyor at the British Works Department, Shanghai. Boyce visited Nagasaki on one or more of his voyages between Shanghai and Yokohama, inspected the consular premises and submitted a report in the form of answers to a questionnaire, dated May 6, 1872.[76] In response to a query about the desirability of repairing the building at No.9 Higashiyamate or erecting a new consulate, he wrote that, "The present building will probably last three to four years, provided the roof be found strong enough... The new building can be erected on the present site with the offices on the lower terrace in the front, provided there is adequate space." With regard to other buildings he commented that, "The consul's private residence with offices attached could be placed upon one lot, but in that case quarters would have to be hired for the assistant as there would not be sufficient room on one lot. I estimate a suitable bungalow could be found for about £120 per annum."

Marcus O. Flowers returned to Nagasaki from home leave in early 1871 and resumed the post of consul. Arthur A. Annesley applied for a promotion but failed the Japan Consular Service examination, which now placed emphasis on ability in the Japanese not Dutch language. One of the first members of the British delegation to Nagasaki in 1859, Annesley had served competently for more than a decade, but his failure in the examination left him little choice but to resign from the Japan Consular Service and to leave Nagasaki with his wife and Nagasaki-born son in September 1871.[77]

British authorities had clearly decided to keep the British consulate at No. 9 Higashiyamate and even to erect new buildings there if necessary. Soon after the above dispatch, the Admiralty (Royal Navy) contacted Marcus O. Flowers asking for advice regarding a potential site for a naval installation in Nagasaki. Flowers responded in a letter dated August 31, 1872 recommending the reserved consular lot at No. 13 Higashiyamate, which he said the British government planned to return to the Japanese government at the end of the year.[78]

Robert H. Boyce had not mentioned the reserved lot in his answers to the above questionnaire, but he brought the subject up in a letter—also dated August 31, 1872 and sent from Nagasaki—to Vice-Admiral Sir Charles Shadwell, commander-in-chief of the Royal Navy's vessels and shore establishments in China.[79] In the letter, he reiterates Flowers' recommend-

[76] "Nagasaki Consulate: Extracts from Mr Boyce's despatch addressed to H. M.'s Charge d'Affairs" (FO262/232/66-7).
[77] Adolphus A. Annesley later served as British consul in Reunion and Portland, Maine. He died in England in 1887.
[78] Marcus O. Flowers to Charles Shadwell, August 31, 1872 (ADM 125/20).
[79] Robert H. Boyce to Charles Shadwell, August 31, 1872 (ADM 125/20).

dation, calling No. 13 Higashiyamate suitable for the use of the Admiralty and even suggesting that steps be taken to acquire the adjacent lot (No. 12 Higashiyamate) and the fine building owned by Walsh, Hall & Co., which had recently moved to Kobe.

The Admiralty briefly acquired the house at No. 10 Higashiyamate but did not apparently make any other effort to install facilities in Nagasaki. The British government meanwhile decided not to renew its title to the reserved consular lot, and both No. 13 and No. 12 Higashiyamate reverted to the control of the Japanese government until being acquired by the Methodist Episcopal Church of America. Members of the Women's Foreign Missionary Society prepared No. 13 Higashiyamate for the construction of a girls' school called Kwassui Jogakkō. The school prospered over the following years and grew into what today is a Nagasaki landmark called Kwassui Women's University.

Marcus O. Flowers remained in Nagasaki until November 1877, when he left the city for Kobe amid a noisy sendoff from both the foreign community and Japanese friends. He had served for eleven years, the longest term of any Nagasaki consul to date. Aside from a few glitches in the consular court, he had skillfully handled a series of crises including attacks on British citizens in the chaotic 1860s, the political catharsis of the Meiji Restoration, and the stubborn government ban on Christianity and persecution of Japanese Christians in the Nagasaki area.[80]

Flowers' successor was James Troup, a graduate of Aberdeen University who had joined the Japan Consular Service as a student interpreter in 1863. Troup continued his predecessor's efforts to improve conditions in the foreign settlement and to promote trade and international exchange, taking charge of not only British but also French, Spanish and Austro-Hungarian interests. He took up residence with his wife and four sons on the second floor of the consulate at No. 9 Higashiyamate, while his assistant, William A. Woolley, lived in a Western-style bungalow at No. 8 Higashiyamate. The building at No. 10 Higashiyamate, acquired for the use of the Admiralty, also remained in British hands. The result was a pocket of British influence perched on the hillside overlooking the rapidly developing commercial district of the Nagasaki Foreign Settlement.

The consular location may have been quiet and scenic, but it provoked displeasure among many British residents and visitors because of its long distance from the waterfront. One debilitated traveler, identifying himself as "Shipmaster," wrote to the local English-language newspaper as follows:

Sir, — Can you inform me why the British Consulate should be situated on

---

[80] Marcus O. Flowers retired from the Japan Consular Service in March 1882 and returned to England, where he died in 1894.

top of a hill right away from the settlement? It may be very pleasant for the Consul and his assistants to sit there all day long and enjoy the breeze, but it is no joke to toil up that hill in the broiling hot sun if you have a little 'pidgin' to put through. I have just returned from the Consulate, with the thermometer 95 in the shade, and the walk up and down has quite unfitted me for work the rest of the day; in fact I am quite knocked up. I think the Consul would do well were he to remove his office somewhere nearer the Settlement. He could luxuriate on the hill after office hours.[81]

The British Foreign Office finally relented and took steps to find a more suitable consular location. Before leaving Nagasaki to take up a new post at Kobe in the spring of 1882, James Troup arranged for the removal of the consulate to No. 6 Ōura, a 614-*tsubo* (2,026 square-meter) lot on the Ōura waterfront. The prominent American trading firm J.C. Frazar & Co. had rented the lot in 1861 and erected a two-story wooden building similar in style to others on the Bund: clapboard walls with shuttered windows painted in pastel colors, a Japanese-style roof covered with ceramic *kawara* tiles, chimneys and coal-burning fireplaces, and a heavy stone surrounding wall. There was also a large stone *godown* (warehouse) at the rear of the property that Troup deemed appropriate for use as a jail, the lack of which at No. 9 Higashiyamate had made it necessary to incarcerate British miscreants in the dark unknown of the Japanese prison in Sakura-machi.

J.C. Frazar & Co. had abandoned Nagasaki for Yokohama, transferring the perpetual lease and selling the buildings at No. 6 Ōura to the British-run Maltby & Co. The latter had closed down soon after the death of its owner Samuel Maltby in 1875, and the property had changed hands several times thereafter. James Troup signed a contract with Charles Sutton, the leaseholder at the time, to rent the building for use as the British consulate from March 1882. The editor of *The Rising Sun and Nagasaki Express* commented on the move as follows:

> The change will doubtless be hailed with satisfaction by all, especially those whose business necessitates their almost daily attendance there; whilst all matters related with shipping will be greatly facilitated by its close proximity to the bay. Part of the large stone godown at the rear of the lot is also to be portioned off and fitted up for a jail, to be used as occasion requires, instead of sending convicted persons to the native jail, as hitherto.[82]

---

[81] *The Nagasaki Times*, August 15, 1868.
[82] *The Rising Sun and Nagasaki Express*, February 4, 1882. The term "godown" was derived from the Malay *godong*.

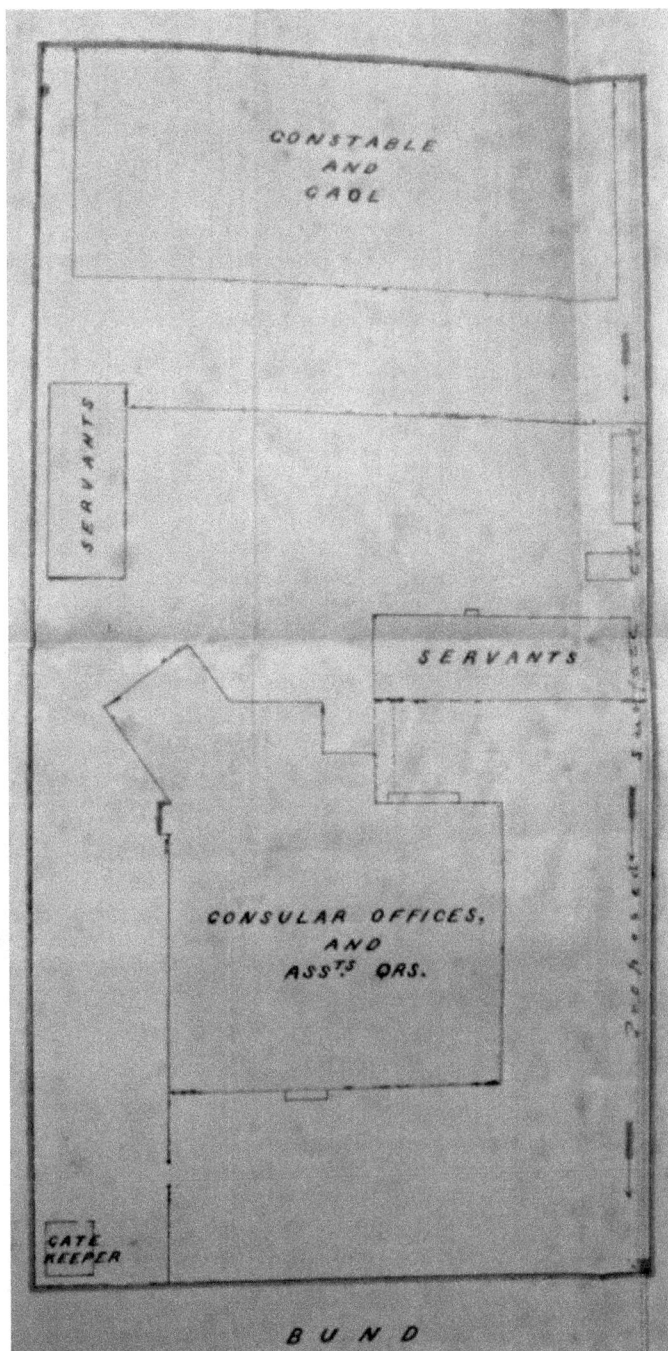

Fig. 3-1 Plan of the buildings comprising the new British Consulate at No. 6 Ōura. The stone warehouse at the rear was converted for use as a jail and residence for the constable. (UK National Archives)

James Troup left Nagasaki for Kobe soon after signing the lease, and John C. Hall arrived to take over as acting consul.[83] After earning a master's degree in law from Queen's College, Belfast, Hall had passed the competitive examination to the Japan Consular Service in 1867 and begun his career the following year as a student interpreter in Tokyo. He moved with his wife and children into the rooms vacated by Troup in the old consulate building. The consular assistant, Henry A. Bonar, remained with his family in the official residence at No. 8 Higashiyamate. At first, the only permanent inhabitants of the new consular premises at No. 6 Ōura were the constable Simeon F. Lawrence and his Japanese wife Yoshi, who lodged in rooms above the jail in the rear of the property. Lawrence had retired from the British army and served for thirteen years as constable at the British consulate in Hakodate before moving to Nagasaki in 1879.

Fig. 3-2 Western-style wooden buildings lined the Nagasaki Bund (from the Anglo-Indian term *bunder* meaning waterfront street) and served as the face of the Nagasaki Foreign Settlement. The Union Jack is flying in front of the British Consulate at No. 6 Ōura. The boat in the foreground is loaded with coal, one of Nagasaki's most important exports. (Private collection)

---

[83] Kuwata, p 474. One of the British delegates involved in the revision of the Anglo-Japanese Treaty in 1895, Troup retired in 1898 and died in England in 1925.

John C. Hall

When John C. Hall and his family reached Nagasaki in 1882, the harbor was scattered with water-going vessels of every size and shape: steamships of various nationalities plying the regular routes linking Japanese, Chinese and Korean ports; Austrian, British and Russian gunboats flying flags of their respective countries; transports, tugs, coal barges, lighters and junks in various states of repair; and hundreds of single-oar sampans ferrying passengers back and forth from the landing steps in front of the custom-house. The city stretched back from the waterfront, to the south the buildings of the foreign settlement and the villas of wealthy foreign residents hidden among trees on the hillsides; to the north, straddling the artificial delta of Nakashima River at the head of the bay, orderly rows of low wooden buildings with ceramic-tile roofs and white paper windows. A grid of flagstone-paved streets led up to a string of Buddhist temples skirting the hillsides and, behind them, graveyards looking out over the old town as if to remind the populace of the impermanence of life.

Although the *chonmage* topknots and samurai swords of old were gone, most of the Japanese people walking in the streets wore traditional dress, lived in houses that dated back to the days before the opening of the port, cooked food with firewood in earthen kitchen *kamado* stoves, illuminated rooms with oil lamps, and enjoyed the same familiar Nagasaki diet spiced with Chinese, Portuguese and Dutch influences. There were no telephone poles, no modern vehicles other than rickshaws with bicycle wheels, no significant military presence, and still very few artifacts of glass or steel to mar the historic townscape. In short, aside from the foreign settlement and its Western-style façades, the physical appearance of Nagasaki and the lifestyles of the people remained mostly unchanged since the end of the Edo Period.

One disturbing problem John C. Hall encountered was Nagasaki's unashamed system of prostitution and the scourge of venereal diseases persisting in its wake. Since the opening of the port in the late 1850s, British and Russian naval officers had made repeated efforts to protect sailors from syphilis and gonorrhea by establishing lock hospitals and urging Japanese authorities to make medical examinations mandatory among prostitutes. As mentioned earlier, Christian missionaries had also joined in the debate, criticizing the Meiji government for failing to rectify the "social evil."

What appalled John C. Hall was not just the indigenous system of prostitution but also the eyesore within the boundaries of the Nagasaki Foreign Settlement, namely the *grog shops* (saloons) that lined the banks of Ōura Creek and catered to the crews of naval vessels and merchant ships. In early 1883, faced with complaints from the Royal Navy and demands from British Minister Harry Parkes, Hall launched an investigation and drew up a list of saloons suspected of harboring prostitutes. In a letter to Parkes in April 1883, he reports the existence of twenty-two public houses in the foreign settlement and states that, "of this number only five are hotels at which board and lodging for travelers is procurable, and of this five only two are fit for respectable people to stop at. The other twenty houses therefore consist of three low-class hotels so-called and seventeen grog shops or taverns."[84] Hall adds that at least ten of the establishments are notorious dens of prostitution, but his efforts to rectify the situation proved mostly ineffective, and his suggestion that the Japanese police be allowed to enter the saloons and arrest offenders fizzled in the face of opposition from other foreign residents.

In December 1883, William G. Aston arrived in Nagasaki to assume the position of consul, and John C. Hall stayed on as assistant. Aston had come to Japan in the final years of the Edo Period as a student interpreter and had served as an assistant at the British Legation in Tokyo and consulates in various treaty ports, winning special commendation for his language ability and progress in studies on Japanese culture and history. He and his wife were welcomed enthusiastically in Nagasaki, but the posting was cut short by an unexpected appointment to serve as acting British consul-general in Korea, the language and customs of which he had also studied. He left Nagasaki in April 1884 and proceeded to Seoul, the first European diplomat to represent his country in the reclusive Hermit Kingdom.[85]

John C. Hall returned to the position of acting consul after Aston's departure, but in a further reshuffling of consular posts at the end of 1884, he was called back to Tokyo to serve as assistant Japanese secretary to the British Legation. Before leaving Nagasaki, he oversaw the purchase of No. 6 Ōura, the property rented since March 1882 for use as the premises of the Nagasaki British Consulate. Charles Sutton agreed to sell the buildings and transfer the perpetual lease to the British government for $2,130 (Mexican silver dollars). The contract signed by Sutton and F.J. Marshall, representative of Her British Majesty's First Commissioner of Works, was dated September 2, 1884.[86]

Hall went on to a distinguished diplomatic career, serving as acting assistant judge of H.B.M. Supreme Court for China and Japan at Shanghai, consul at Kobe, and consul-general at Yokohama. He received a Coronation

---

[84] J.C. Hall to Harry Parkes, April 27, 1883 (FO 262/404).

[85] *The Rising Sun and Nagasaki Express*, April 19, 1884. William G. Aston returned to Tokyo the following year to serve as secretary to the British Legation. Poor health forced him to retire from the Japan Consular Service and retire to England in 1889, but he went on to publish the first English translation of the Japanese classic *Nihongi* and numerous other books and articles on Japanese and Korean subjects before his death in 1911. He is remembered today as one of the foremost British Japanologists of the nineteenth century.

[86] FO 262/423/130.

Medal (1911) and the Order of St Michael and St George for important non-military service overseas (1912) prior to his retirement in 1914.[87]

Masonic Lodge

John C. Hall's successor was James J. Enslie, the son of an admiral in the Dutch Navy and fluent Dutch speaker who had entered the Japan Consular Service as an interpreter at Nagasaki in 1861. He had gained the trust and admiration of both his British colleagues and Japanese associates over the course of subsequent appointments, including vice-consul at Kobe and Osaka, acting registrar and crown prosecutor in Japan and acting consul at Yokohama. Granted a special housing allowance in Nagasaki, Enslie and his wife took up residence at No. 33 Minamiyamate, a hillside lot commanding a panoramic view of the harbor at the southern extremity of the foreign settlement. His assistant, a young student interpreter named Arthur M. Chalmers, inhabited rooms in the main building at No. 6 Ōura.

In December 1885, Enslie posted a notice in *The Rising Sun and Nagasaki Express* announcing the sale of the former consulate premises at No. 8 and No. 9 Higashiyamate, as well as the house at No. 10 Higashiyamate no longer needed for the Royal Navy.[88] Signed by F.J. Marshall, the notice states that "the buildings comprise a six-roomed bungalow, with out-offices, on lots 8 and 10, and a two-storied house of eight rooms on lot 9" and that the land rent due to the Japanese government had been paid to March 31, 1886. In a follow-up article published on January 30, 1886, the newspaper reported that lots No. 9 and No. 10 had been sold at public auction for $510 and $150, respectively. The buyer, the Reformed Church in America, planned to open a school for boys on the site and to build houses for missionaries. The lease to No. 8 Higashiyamate was returned to the Japanese authorities at the end of March but acquired shortly thereafter by the same Church and incorporated into a mission school complex called Steele Academy (Tōzan Gakuin).

Now the old wooden building and stone warehouses at No. 6 Ōura comprised the sole hub of British diplomacy in Nagasaki, flying the Union Jack conspicuously on a flagstaff in the front garden in full view of passersby and ships entering the harbor.

Enslie's dispatches to Japanese officials reflect the cordial relationship between British and Japanese officials in the mid-1880s and the peaceful, albeit economically sluggish, atmosphere of the Nagasaki Foreign Settlement. Many are requests forwarded from British residents and travelers for permission to leave the confines of the settlement and to visit the famous hot

---

[87] Kuwata, p. 286.
[88] *The Rising Sun and Nagasaki Express*, December 19, 1885.

springs in Hizen and Shimabara. The reason given was usually "health improvement," which in practical terms could mean anything from refreshing dips in mineral baths to flings with *geisha*, picnics and hunting expeditions. Some of the other dispatches are applications for Japanese cooperation in solving mundane problems such as potholes in the flagstone paths of the settlement and the odor emanating from uncollected garbage— and the subsequent letters of thanks. In one note, Enslie asked the governor of Nagasaki Prefecture to convey his thanks to the commanders of the Imperial Japanese Navy warships *Ryūjo* and *Mujo* for their consideration in following the example of British warships and lowering their flags to half-mast to mark the death of former British Minister Harry Parkes.[89]

James J. Enslie was also one of the founding members of the Nagasaki Masonic Lodge. In early 1885, he and a number of other Freemasons residing in Nagasaki applied to the Grand Masonic Lodge of Scotland for permission to establish a local lodge. Permission granted, the initial group of sixteen members, including British engineers employed at the Mitsubishi Nagasaki Shipyard and *The Rising Sun and Nagasaki Express* editor Arthur Norman, gathered for the first meeting of the Nagasaki Masonic Lodge No. 710 S.C. on October 5, 1885. By the time the lodge moved to the upper story of Norman's printing shop at No. 47 Sagarimatsu in June 1887, the number of members had increased almost twofold.[90]

On the eve of James J. Enslie's departure for a new posting as consul at Kobe in February 1889, a large group of Nagasaki inhabitants, including fellow Freemasons, foreign residents and their families and Japanese friends, held a farewell party to express gratitude for his various contributions. Leading British merchant Frederick Ringer read a letter of gratitude, and Enslie responded with the comment that: "It is a source of intense satisfaction to me to see assembled here such a large number of my Japanese and foreign friends, whilst the fact that so very many ladies grace this entertainment is an honour of which I am deeply sensible; and the names of so many reverend gentlemen being appended to the address just now read is proof positive that in Nagasaki we are, as a community, one in thought and feelings."[91]

---

[89] J.J. Enslie to Ishida Yeikichi, March 24, 1885 (*Raikan*, 1885).
[90] The Nagasaki Masonic Lodge lost momentum with the decline in Nagasaki's fortunes as an international port after the Russo-Japanese War (1904-5) and was declared dormant in 1919. All that remains today is a few gravestones inscribed with the ruler and compass insignia and the former gate at No. 47 Sagarimatsu, relocated to Glover Garden after World War Two.
[91] *The Rising Sun and Nagasaki Express*, February 27, 1889. James J. Enslie died of a chronic illness on June 14, 1896 and was buried in the Kobe Foreign Cemetery.

Continuing Troubles in the Consular Court

John J. Quin returned to Nagasaki in early 1889 to succeed James J. Enslie. The native of Ireland had passed the Japan Consular Service examination in 1867 and served as an assistant at Yokohama and Nagasaki before his promotion to consul at Hakodate in 1886. In the interim, he had won acclaim for his scholarly research on traditional Japanese *shikki* (lacquerware) and had amassed a much-admired personal collection. Both his official report submitted while serving as acting consul at Hakodate in 1882 and his dissertation entitled *The Lacquer Industry of Japan* published in the Transactions of the Asiatic Society of Japan called attention to the beauty of the traditional art and remain to the present day as essential English-language works on the subject.[92]

Fig.3-3 The Ōura Bund (waterfront street) circa 1890. The office of Holme, Ringer & Co. is on the far right. Beside it, with the tall flagstaff, is the Nagasaki British Consulate, still ensconced in the old buildings dating back to the 1860s. (Private collection)

John J. Quin achieved various advances in studies related to Japanese culture, but his record in the Nagasaki consular court was not quite as illustrious. In March 1890, F.D. Nelson, chief engineer on the British steamship *Felbridge*, wrote a long letter to *The Rising Sun and Nagasaki Express*

---

[92] Hew D.V. Prendergast, Helena Jaeschke, and Naomi Rumball, *A Lacquer Legacy at Kew: The Japanese Collection of John J. Quin* (University of Chicago Press, 2001).

complaining about an alleged injustice at the hands of John J. Quin in the Nagasaki consular court. Nelson reported that a steward on his ship had insulted and tried to strike him, whereupon he hit back in self defense and knocked the man to the floor. The latter filed a complaint at the British consulate, and Quin ordered the parties to appear in the consular court. Nelson, accompanied by the captain and second officer of the ship, went to the consulate as instructed, but the steward failed to appear, and Quin officially dismissed the case. Nelson was walking back along the waterfront when he received a message calling him back to the consulate, Quin having changed his mind. The steward, who had appeared belatedly without any other witness, swore that Nelson had been the aggressor, while the chief engineer's testimony was verified by both the captain and second officer. Says Nelson:

> You, and all who read this, my judge of my amazement when the gentleman whose turn it has, by rotation, been to preside over the destinies of troubled British, Austro-Hungarian and Spanish subjects here, gave his decision in the matter by fining me the sum of five dollars and costs! I, of course, protested and refused to pay, but the captain being anxious not to have any further trouble, I paid the amount, as other sums have been paid before, under protest. The consequence to me was that I came away from the court a wiser, but not by any means a better man: wiser in that I had learned what amount of confidence to put in a consular court in the future; not better, morally, in that I had inwardly decided to take my change out of the steward at the first opportunity. [93]

No further mention of the case appeared in the newspaper or consular records, but it was clear to the foreign residents of Nagasaki and other Japanese ports that the arbitrary sentences passed down in consular courts, like the system of extraterritoriality, were no longer tolerable.

The Problem of Merchant Consuls

The 1890 issue of the *Nagasaki Directory* lists the presence of thirteen foreign consular delegations in Nagasaki. Officially-appointed consuls ensconced in independent premises within the Nagasaki Foreign Settlement headed five of the thirteen delegations, that is, China, Germany, Great Britain, Russia and the United States. Of the remaining eight, three were represented by one of the above official consuls and five by foreign businessmen or *merchant consuls* residing in Nagasaki and engaged in commercial activities linked to the relevant country.

---

[93] *The Rising Sun and Nagasaki Express*, March 12, 1890.

The most prominent and influential merchant consul was Frederick Ringer, head of the British trade and shipping agency Holme, Ringer & Co. In December 1882, Ringer had accepted a request from the government of Belgium to handle that country's interests in the port. His partner John C. Smith accepted a similar request from Denmark the same year. The appointments stemmed from business connections and the desire of the respective countries to avoid the expense of an official consulate, but in practical terms they placed Ringer and Smith, not merely on an equal footing with the British consul and his counterparts, but in fact above them because hierarchy among the consuls was decided on the basis of length of stay. When one of the partners left Nagasaki for an extended period, he named the other as acting-consul and thereby maintained diplomatic ascendancy.

Signing himself "His Belgian Majesty's Consul and Senior Consul," Frederick Ringer wrote directly to the governor of Nagasaki Prefecture at the end of 1889 asking for help in bringing about a number of improvements urgently needed in the foreign settlement. He seemed to be speaking for the entire consular body, including John J. Quin, but the British consul later submitted the following protest to the governor of Nagasaki Prefecture, clearly disgruntled at finding himself outranked by a merchant of his own nationality:

> I have the honor to inform you that as I am of the opinion that the seniority among the members of the foreign consular body at this port should rest solely among the officially paid consuls, and not with the unpaid merchant consuls, it is not my intention in the future to recognize Mr. Ringer, Belgian consul, as senior consul, nor any other merchant consul who may so designate himself. I shall not therefore attend any consular meetings called either by him, or any other merchant consul, nor be present at any official meeting or reception where such seniority is accorded to him. In the future, therefore, I beg that should you at any time desire my decision upon any matter of general consular interest that you will address me separately on the subject, when I shall be most happy to give the matter my most careful attention and consideration.[94]

His opinion was reiterated by John C. Hall, who came back to Nagasaki in 1890 to take over as British consul during John J. Quin's leave of absence. Hall rejected Frederick Ringer's seniority and even wrote a long letter to his superior in Tokyo complaining about the blatant undermining of his authority. The resentful consul insisted that merchants are viewed with much less respect in Japan than in Western countries and therefore that the merchant consul is inherently disadvantaged in dealings with local government. He reported that when he took office he found Frederick

---

[94] J.J. Quin to Nakano Tateakira, June 19, 1890 (*Raikan*, 1890).

Ringer serving as senior consul and usurping his role as leader of the foreign community in social events. Finally, he implored the British envoy to communicate with the governments of Belgium and Denmark and to urge them to demote Ringer and Smith to the innocuous position of vice-consuls.[95]

Frederick Ringer and John C. Smith eventually acquiesced for the sake of peaceful coexistence and allowed whoever among the British, American, Russian and German consuls held seniority to fill the role of official representative of the foreign community. But the fact remained that the professional consuls served on the short term and played a mostly ceremonial role, while the doyens of Holme, Ringer & Co. maintained close alliances with influential members of the Japanese community and tightened their grip on economic and social affairs in the foreign settlement.

Among various other undertakings, Ringer served as Nagasaki agent for the Canadian Pacific Railway (CPR) Company, a government-subsidized organization formed to lay tracks across the expanses of the Dominion of Canada and to provide a fast connection between London and the ports of East Asia. After the transcontinental railway reached completion in 1886, the company chartered three steamships from the Cunard Line and started a regular service from Hong Kong to Vancouver via Shanghai, Nagasaki, Kobe and Yokohama. The *Abyssinia* reached Vancouver for the first time in June 1887 carrying a load of tea and silk that was promptly transferred onto boxcars and shipped eastward.

The undertaking was so successful that the CPR ordered three new 6,000-ton sail-rigged steamships from the Naval Construction and Armaments Company, Barrow, England, in October 1888. The *Empress of India* left Liverpool on its maiden voyage in early February 1891 and followed the old route to Japan via the Suez Canal, reaching Nagasaki on the morning of April 12, 1891.

The *Empress of India* called regularly at Nagasaki from 1891 to 1914. Along with its sister ships the *Empress of Japan* and *Empress of China*, the sleek three-mast steamship plied the route from Hong Kong to Vancouver, breaking records for speed across the Pacific Ocean and setting new standards for luxurious international travel. Now travelers could circle the globe without ever leaving British territory, following the *all-red route* so called because British colonies and common-wealth countries were colored red on maps. The Nagasaki British Consulate, meanwhile, became a node on the vast commercial and cultural network of the British Empire and a symbol of British-Japanese cooperation in East Asia.

---

[95] J.C. Hall to Hugh Fraser (H.B.M. Envoy Extraordinary), January 11, 1892 (FO 262/679).

4 AT THE TURN OF THE CENTURY

IN THE SUMMER OF 1894, the Japanese ambassador to Britain and his British counterpart agreed to revise the Anglo-Japanese Treaty in force since 1858. Signed on July 16, the new Treaty of Commerce and Navigation between Japan and Great Britain called for an end to the system of extraterritoriality and set a precedent for similar treaty revisions by the United States, France and other countries. The announcement provoked an outcry from a few foreign residents concerned that the new treaties would jeopardize their business interests and exclusive social position in Japan. However, the Japanese government promised to honor the perpetual leases issued during the foreign settlement period and to guarantee the rights of foreigners to travel, live and do business anywhere they wanted in Japan. Effective July 1899, the new treaties rectified the imbalances inherent in the former treaties and brought Japan onto an equal footing with the Western powers.

The ink had barely dried on the treaty document when an armed conflict broke out between Japan and China. The two countries declared war on August 1, 1894 over conflicting interests in Korea and leapt into a bloodbath on land and sea. The Japanese forces quickly predominated, demonstrating Japan's newfound military prowess and industrial capacity and sending ripples of surprise around the world. In the Treaty of Shimonoseki signed by the two countries on April 17, 1895, China agreed to recognize Korean independence and to cede Formosa (Taiwan) and the Pescadores Islands to Japan. Japanese companies gained the right to operate ships on the Yangtze River and establish manufacturing facilities in Shanghai and other ports. The treaty precipitated a sharp boost in shipping in the waters of northeast Asia and further colonial incursions in China by foreign powers.

The involvement of the British Foreign Office in the region deepened in concert with the expansion of Japan's territorial holdings and sphere of influence in East Asia. In addition to the traditional postings in Tokyo and the former treaty ports of Yokohama, Kobe, Osaka, Hakodate and Nagasaki, the Japan Consular Service dispatched diplomats to Chemulpo and Seoul (Korea), Dairen (China), Tainan and Tamsui (Formosa), Manila (Philippines) and Shimonoseki, while at the same time employing prominent British residents in several smaller ports to handle the duties related to communication with Japanese officials and the administration of British interests.

Only a day and a night from Shanghai and Dairen, Nagasaki experienced an unprecedented boom as a coal depot, supply harbor and rest place for foreign warships and merchantmen. In February 1896, the local English-language newspaper reported that:

> During the year 1895 no less than 160 different men-of-war of all nationalities visited Nagasaki. Of course the number of men-of-war entries is much greater, some of them coming here as many as five or six times during the twelve months. And large as these numbers are, those of this year give every indication of being larger, the large increase in the Far-Eastern fleets of the Powers and disturbed state of the political atmosphere being the prime factors in bringing this about.[96]

The increase in harbor traffic naturally resulted in an economic windfall for the people of Nagasaki, filling the coffers of suppliers and trading companies and lining the pockets of all the people, Japanese and foreign, involved in business and transportation.

Despite the good news in Nagasaki, John J. Quin fell ill and decided to go on furlough, leaving his assistant, Ralph G.E. Forster, to serve as acting British consul. He apparently intended to return to the post after convalescing in his native land, but he announced his retirement from the Japan Consular Service in November 1896 and died at his brother's residence in Kingstown, Ireland in February the following year.

Joseph H. Longford replaced John J. Quin as Nagasaki consul in July 1897. Longford had arrived in Japan as a student interpreter and risen through the ranks of the Japan Consular Service as one of its brightest stars, serving as the first British consul in Formosa (Taiwan) after the cession of the island to Japan in the wake of the Sino-Japanese War. During his stay in Nagasaki, Longford lived with his wife and four children in the Glover house at No. 3 Minamiyamate—the fabled *Ipponmatsu*—and later the two-story house at No. 15 Minamiyamate, both of which commanded a panoramic view over Nagasaki Harbor and remain to this day.

In a report on trade and navigation in Nagasaki during the year 1896,

---

[96] *The Nagasaki Shipping List*, February 21, 1896.

Longford describes the boom in international business and expresses optimism about the future of the port:

Nagasaki is, of all Eastern ports, perhaps that which is most frequented by foreign men-of-war of all nationalities, and it would not be an excessive estimate to say that fully $1,000,000 are annually spent in the port by their crews and on the purchase of supplies, a great portion of which goes into Japanese hands, directly or indirectly. Large sums are also disbursed by mail and other merchant steamers for supplies, and by tourists and other temporary residents, especially by Russians, large numbers of whom from Vladivostok are now making the port a winter residence. But in addition to Nagasaki there are other ports which furnish an outlet for the productions of Southern Japan, the principal being Shimonoseki, Moji, and Kuchinotsu, and all three may be considered as subsidiary ports to Nagasaki… With the single exception of the French, all lines of mail steamers now running to the East call at Nagasaki both on their outward and inward voyages, and this is the only port of call either in China or Japan of the magnificent vessels of the Russian Volunteer Fleet. The preponderance and advance of British shipping are both very marked. The number of British vessels that entered Nagasaki in 1896 was 335 and the tonnage 746,130, and the total entered both in Nagasaki and the subsidiary ports, 722 vessels of 1,582,479 tonnes… The Island of Formosa has not yet answered the expectations formed of it by the Japanese, but in whatever wealth it may ultimately bring to Japan, Nagasaki as the nearest port must have a large share, while the opening of the Siberian Railway must also tend greatly to its advantage, and from its proximity to the Pacific terminus of the railway, give it also a large share in whatever trade Japan may develop with Siberia.[97]

Longford's lengthy report on affairs in Nagasaki the following year was not only submitted to the Foreign Office but also published in two consecutive issues of *The Nagasaki Press* for the information of the local community.[98] In the report, the consul continues his analysis of trends in trade and industry and comments on the remarkable increase in commercial activity in the port, attributing it to factors such as the selection of Nagasaki as a regular port-of-call for the warships of the Russian East Asian Fleet and the American Navy, the increased colonial presence in northeastern China, the popularity of Nagasaki as a tourist destination, and the impending extension of the national railway system to the port. Says Longford: "During the course of ten years the value in local currency of the aggregate trade of the southern district of Japan has grown over threefold. Practically, Nagasaki

---

[97] 'Report on the Trade and Navigation of Nagasaki for 1896', quoted in full in *The Nagasaki Press*, December 8-9, 1897.
[98] *The Nagasaki Press*, October 28 and 29, 1898.

may be taken as the sole seat of the import trade, and this has increased over sixfold." He also points out that the value of imports from Britain accounted for no less than 65% of the total, figures that reflect both the predominance of British enterprises in the Nagasaki Foreign Settlement and the importance of the British consulate as a nerve center in the port.

Fig.4-1 Nagasaki Harbor strewn with foreign steamships around the turn of the twentieth century. The building on the lower right is the Belle Vue Hotel, premises of the Nagasaki British Consulate from 1862 to 1864. (Private collection)

Retirement of Simeon F. Lawrence

At the end of 1898, Joseph H. Longford wrote a letter to Ernest Satow, the British minister in Tokyo, reporting that Simeon F. Lawrence had been forced by illness to retire and requesting Satow's intervention in securing a generous government pension for the elderly British resident, who had been serving as constable at the Nagasaki consulate since 1879. Longford describes Lawrence as "a most efficient public servant in every way" and points out that he had "been for over 43 years almost continuously in her Majesty's service, this long period having been broken for only two years (1864-66), during which he was employed as a municipal policeman in Yokohama."[99]

---

[99] J.H. Longford to Sir Ernest Satow, December 29, 1898 (FO 262/792). Simeon F.

Indeed, Simeon F. Lawrence, like Sir Ernest Satow, was one of the longest-running employees of the Japan Consular Service.

In a follow-up letter early the next year, Longford informs Satow that he has hired a new constable in Nagasaki on a six-month contract, pending instructions from the Foreign Office regarding Lawrence's successor. He notes that many of the duties performed by the constable to date, such as the arrest and incarceration of wrongdoers, would be eliminated by the treaty revisions due to take force in July 1899. On the other hand, however, he points out that Simeon F. Lawrence had also handled a number of administrative tasks that remained important and would have to be entrusted to a British employee. Longford goes on to provide a long list of official duties, information that sheds a fascinating light on the activities of the British consulate around the turn of the century:

> All the shipping work was carried out by Constable Lawrence and shipping papers signed by him, in both cases with the exceptions hereafter noted. This included entry and clearance of ships, engagement and discharge of seamen, examinations of accounts of wages on discharge, preparations of Bills of Health and notes of protest, warrants of arrest and applications to local authorities for arrest, all these being signed by myself, supervision of distressed seamen while in consulate charge and arrangements for their conveyance elsewhere, settlement of petty squabbles between masters and seamen, sale of effects of deceased seamen, keeping and preparation of Board of Trade accounts and issue of fee stamps in all shipping services...
>
> Other services performed by Lawrence were: general charge of the buildings and compound and supervision of repairs on account of the Office of Works; supervision of servants and payment of their wages, a duty which though easy enough formerly when civil trustworthy servants contentedly continued in their employment for many years, rendered quite the reverse by the new manners and customs of the Japanese lower orders; keeping the petty cash accounts, postage and incidentals; registration of British subjects and the issue of passports (both registration certificates and passports being, however, signed by myself)...
>
> The Board of Trade duties exclusively discharged by the assistant or myself are preparation of casualty returns, inquiries into and reports and returns of death on board ship, extensions of protests, all connected with naval courts, and the sale of ships, issue of provisional certificates of registry, surveys, examination of and entries in official logs, certificates of change of masters, and others which do not occur to me at the moment. All serious disputes between masters and men are investigated by myself.

Lawrence died in Nagasaki on September 26, 1902 at the age of sixty-four. Yoshi Lawrence died in 1912 and was buried along with her husband at Sakamoto International Cemetery, where their gravestone can still be seen today.

These are both frequent and troublesome at this port, cases occurring where nearly the whole crew of one ship will appear angrily claiming their discharges, and I never allow them to come into court except as a very last resort when every effort at reconciliation has failed or in cases of most incorrigible misconduct. With the exception of officers or men transferred from one mail steamer to another of the same company, every case of discharge is also inquired into by myself before it is sanctioned.

As to the duties discharged by the constable which may be said to strictly belong to his office, the principal are the custody of the jail in which there were last week, for example, eleven prisoners, assisting masters in procuring seamen to fill vacancies in their crews or to find deserters or absentees before sailing, conveying discharged prisoners on board their ships, soothing truculent and noisy seamen in the office, and in regard to the navy the receipt, care, and forwarding of Admiralty mail bags. The first of these will, I presume, come to an entire end on the expiration of extraterritoriality. A very valuable service was also rendered by Lawrence in arranging disputes or quarrels between seamen of the navy and natives. He was well known to naval seamen, his age and character enabled him to exercise great influence over them, and I may say he also exercised great influence over settlement coolies and boatmen, to all of whom he was also well known. The local police frequently applied to him for assistance in the first stages of a threatening row, and his timely and tactful interference has in scores of cases prevented what might easily have become a serious disturbance.[100]

In the letter, Joseph H. Longford offers his opinion regarding the best way to deal with the duties handled to date by the constable. He responds positively to Ernest Satow's suggestion that one of the constables currently employed in Yokohama could be persuaded to accept a transfer to Nagasaki. As it turned out, an unnamed constable was hired temporarily in the wake of Simeon F. Lawrence's retirement but dismissed after the completion of his six-month contract, and George Kircher, the former second constable at Yokohama, was employed in the Nagasaki consulate as of November 1, 1899. At this juncture, Ernest Satow and his colleagues decided to do away with "constable" and to apply the title "shipping clerk" to the new position in consulates throughout Japan.

The End of Extraterritoriality

The treaty revisions agreed upon by Japan and the Western powers came into effect in July 1899, effectuating the abolition of the foreign settlements as separate legal entities and the restoration of Japan's autonomy in customs

---

[100] J.H. Longford to Sir Ernest Satow, February 2, 1899 (FO 262/818).

tariffs, immigration and diplomatic affairs. The cosignatories agreed that the privilege of extraterritoriality would be rescinded but that, until they were given up voluntarily by their foreign holders, the perpetual leases currently in effect in the foreign settlements would be honored by the Japanese government. While Japan guaranteed the rights of foreigners to travel, live, and do business anywhere they wanted in Japan, the foreign powers agreed to recognize Japan as an equal sovereign state, to exchange ambassadors and to follow the rule of Japanese law.

Many foreign residents of the former treaty ports were opposed to any change in the status quo because it threatened their long-standing financial and legal privileges and jeopardized their cherished sense of superiority, an illusion fostered by the colonial system in which foreigners kept *natives* and their supposedly primitive cultures at bay. Cries of apprehension began to echo in the streets of the foreign settlements soon after the announcement of treaty revisions and continued over the months leading up to the momentous change:

> That this uneasiness is not without reason may easily be understood by those who have had any experience of Japanese customs. It has been the fashion, and therefore a stupid conventionality, of late to extol the virtues of Japanese institutions and undoubtedly these are not without their points. But Japan as a nation is still too vexed and restricted in her progress by truly Oriental survivals to be given dominion over Europeans, their lives and properties. By this, it will, we are sure, be understood we do not intend any reproach to the Mikado's Government, nor do we ignore the humanity of the motives by which the Japanese as a people are generally inspired. But we do hold, and insist, that until the laws and institutions of her land shall have more nearly approximated to our own, British subjects, and for that matter all Europeans, should be permitted to enjoy the boon of extraterritoriality.[101]

The change in Japan's relationship with the world and the status of foreigners living there arrived on July 17, 1899 in keeping with the new treaties, and most observers welcomed the change as a correction of previous imbalances and an opportunity for progress on both sides. Wrote the editor of *The Nagasaki Press*:

> To-day, the 17th of July, marks an epoch in the history of Japan, a country that has already surprised the Occident by its wonderful adaptation in so short a time to the modern civilization of the Western world. After years of patient toiling on the part of her able statesmen, Japan to-day enters

---

[101] *Consular Journal of Greater Britain* (September 8, 1898), quoted in *The Nagasaki Press*, October 20, 1898.

upon an equal footing with all the Powers, and now holds the proud distinction of being the first Oriental nation to exercise jurisdiction over Occidentals. The old Treaties have ceased to exist, and there is reason to believe that under the new order of things foreigners resident in this country, and those who come after, will have little to fear from the change.

For the majority of foreign residents, the only negative impact in fact was the annoyance of having to apply for business licenses at city hall.[102] The perpetual leases on residential and business properties were acknowledged by the Japanese government under the new system, the Japanese laws that foreigners were now obliged to observe were essentially the same as those in force hitherto, and no change was apparent in the attitude of the Japanese police toward foreigners. The lack of any special celebration of the event in Nagasaki or discussion of its significance in the local newspapers suggests that Japanese people also expected relationships with foreigners to remain unchanged and business to go on as usual. More than anything else, the ports of Nagasaki, Kobe and Yokohama were riding a wave of prosperity high enough to eclipse concerns about the future.

Thus, although legally abolished, the Nagasaki Foreign Settlement persisted as an unofficial institution retaining its primarily foreign population, its unique social infrastructure and quasi-Western architectural identity, and, for the foreigners who lived there, the neighborhoods of Higashiyamate and Minamiyamate continued to provide a safe gray zone neither really in Japan nor out, a refuge from both the inscrutable world of Japanese culture and the pigeon holes of life back home.

However, the revision of the old treaties held enormous significance for Japanese leaders watching global affairs from Tokyo, a fact evidenced by the promulgation—almost simultaneously with the treaty revisions—of the Strategic Zone Law (*yōsai chitai hō*). Enacted in August 1899, the new law designated a number of cities around the country as high-security zones, Nagasaki near the top of the list because of its proximity to the continent. Government officials called for the stationing of a battalion of the Sasebo Fortress Artillery Regiment in the Takenokubo neighborhood of the city under the name *Nagasaki yōsai shireibu* (Nagasaki Fortress Headquarters).

One of the clauses in the law was a strict ban on the measurement and photography of the city, harbor and environs, a restriction that jarred sharply with Nagasaki's former liberality. The ban brought an abrupt end to the history of panoramic photography in Nagasaki dating back to the end of the Edo Period when photographers like Pierre Rossier, Felix Beato and Ueno

---

[102] For a complete list of the businesses required to submit forms, see *Kyoryūchi tekkyo junbisho*, (List of Preparations for the Removal of the Foreign Settlement), Nagasaki Museum of History and Culture (14-554-3).

Hikoma immortalized scenes of the port and city emerging from the mist of national seclusion. After 1899, all photographs of Nagasaki and environs had to be altered so as to hide the line of mountains and avoid showing any military or industrial facility.

Matsuyebashidori Oura, Nagasaki 　リ 通 橋 江 松 浦 大 崎 長

Fig.4-2 A picture postcard shows the main street running through the Ōura commercial district of the Nagasaki Foreign Settlement circa 1910, looking south toward Benten Bridge. The line of the mountain in the background is deliberately obscured. (Private collection)

Plans for a New Consulate Building

While Nagasaki surged ahead economically, the old consulate buildings at No. 6 Ōura became increasingly shabby and unfit as an enclave for Her British Majesty's representatives in western Japan. As early as the summer of 1898, Joseph H. Longford was writing to British authorities in Tokyo asking for money to fund projects such as the installation of equipment to connect the consulate with the city water mains and the construction of a separate entrance to living quarters to assure the privacy of the assistant and his family. He also reported that British architect William Cowan, Her Majesty's Surveyor of Works in Shanghai, had visited the Nagasaki consulate and ordered the painting of the old building and a number of other repairs.[103]

---

[103] J.H. Longford to Sir Ernest Satow, August 30, 1898 (FO 262/792).

By 1901, the appeals for modifications were giving way to expressions of agreement that Nagasaki's vibrant economy justified the complete reconstruction of buildings. Before returning to England on a leave of absence in April the same year, Joseph H. Longford wrote to the British ambassador in Tokyo about the state of the consulate and its prospects for the future. In the letter, he points out that the buildings are of "great age" and that rebuilding "must be taken into consideration within a few years," and he goes on to comment that, although the property was acquired for only $2,130 in 1884:

> The land alone, if offered for sale, would no doubt now speedily find a purchaser for one hundred thousand yen and its value is yearly increasing, so that the Office of Works has on the whole thoroughly good reason to be satisfied with its investment... Nagasaki has become one of the greatest shipping and naval ports in the East; all of its inhabitants, both foreign and native, are full of confidence for the future, and should rebuilding be undertaken, it is hoped that it will be done on a scale commensurate with the profit already made by the Office of Works, the rising importance of the town, and the excellent site, one of the most commanding and convenient in the place.[104]

Longford was expected to return to his post after the leave of absence, but he surprised his colleagues by announcing his retirement and accepting an appointment as first professor of Japanese at King's College London.[105] Ralph G.E. Forster, who had taken over as acting consul, left Nagasaki for a new posting in Hakodate in October 1902 and was replaced by E. Hamilton Holmes, a member of the Japan Consular Service since 1897 and still only twenty-six years old at the time of his move to Nagasaki.

The same month, William Cowan wrote to the Office of Works in London reiterating his opinion that the time had come to rebuild the consular premises in Nagasaki:

> The violent typhoons and seismic disturbances that are so frequent in Japan make the buildings not altogether safe, and collapse might be anticipated should either be a little more violent than usual. The stone built godown was formerly partly used for constable's quarters and gaol, but a consular gaol being no longer necessary in Japan, this building must also be pulled down to give space for the new quarters required for shipping clerk and official servants. At present the consul receives a house allowance from the

---

[104] J.H. Longford to Sir Claude MacDonald, April 23, 1901 (FO 262/855).
[105] Longford devoted his life to studies on Japan after leaving the consular service. He published several scholarly papers and books, including *The Story of Old Japan* (1910) and *Japan of the Japanese* (1911). (Kuwata, pp 341-2)

Foreign Office, but the house to be provided can be made sufficient for a consul, and the assistant can have a house allowance if desired. The costs of these buildings are mentioned in my estimates for 1903/4 at Yen 48,000.[106]

Cowan's proposal remained on hold until the summer of 1904, when E. Hamilton Holmes wrote to the British Embassy in Tokyo calling attention to the rundown condition of the consulate, finally reporting in September that the danger of collapse had become so acute that temporary offices were urgently required.[107] He informs the ambassador that he consulted with the local manager of the American-run China and Japan Trading Company about the rental, for 75 yen per month, of a two-story building at No. 47 Sagarimatsu formerly used by the Chinese Eastern Railway Company, "being situated on the Bund in a central position and consisting of two large rooms at the front, suitable for Consul's and shipping offices, and two smaller ones, with spacious outhouses, and quarters above in which the shipping clerk could reside." In a follow-up dated October 10, he reports that he removed the consulate to No. 47 Sagarimatsu two days earlier and boarded up the old buildings at No. 6 Ōura pending instructions from the Office of Works.

Lot No. 47 Sagarimatsu faced the harbor in the southern part of the former Nagasaki Foreign Settlement. Built in the early Meiji Period, the Western-style building had served over the years as the residence of British shipchandler Charles Sutton (the former leaseholder of the British consulate property at No. 6 Ōura) and later the office of the English-language newspaper *The Rising Sun and Nagasaki Express*. Arthur Norman, the editor of the newspaper, had rented the upper story to the Nagasaki Masonic Lodge for a number of years, and the gate bearing the Freemason's symbol was still standing at the entrance.

William Cowan wrote to the Office of Works again the following month, reporting that he had inspected the old buildings at No. 6 Ōura and decided that they needed to be demolished immediately because of the threat of damage to neighboring properties, adding that: "Endeavors have been made to dispose of the building as old material, but no reasonable offer could be obtained; a contract has therefore been made to take down and store the materials on the site for Yen 200 (£20)."[108]

---

[106] William Cowan to the Secretary of the Office of Works, October 11, 1902 (WORK 10/359).
[107] E.H. Holmes to Sir Claude MacDonald, September 30, 1904 (FO 262/917).
[108] William Cowan to the Office of Works, November 4, 1904 (WORK 10/359).

In the Wake of the Russo-Japanese War

E. Hamilton Holmes managed the Nagasaki British Consulate until January 1905, when Frank W. Playfair arrived in Nagasaki to officially succeed Joseph H. Longford.[109] Playfair had climbed the ladder of the Japan Consular Service since his appointment as a student interpreter in 1880, filling a series of posts as assistant and acting consul until his promotion to consul at Hakodate in 1898 and transfer to the newly opened Shimonoseki consulate in 1901. His move to Nagasaki came at the height of the Russo-Japanese War, a conflict that cemented British-Japanese military and political relationships but spelt hard times for the people of Nagasaki because it brought trade and shipping to a virtual standstill.

For centuries, proximity to the continent had made Nagasaki a commercial gateway and "window to the world;" now it meant only strategic importance in Japan's military collision with Russia.

War broke out between Japan and Russia in the early months of 1904. The number of steamships arriving in Nagasaki dwindled day by day until February 20 when the English-language newspapers—probably for the first time in their more than forty-year history—printed the word NONE in the arrivals column of the shipping intelligence section. Companies run by Russians or involved in business with Russia, such as M. Ginsburg & Co., N. Mess & Co. and the Russo-Chinese Bank, closed their Nagasaki offices or transferred their agencies to British firms, and the Russian consul and other Russian residents boarded ships and hastily returned to their country. Hotel rooms, restaurant tables and bar counters in the former foreign settlement lay vacant, and the flow of business in the Japanese town froze up under the constraints of martial law and the added burden of war taxes.

Despite the sudden downturn in Nagasaki's fortunes as an international port, the British government pressed forward with the plan to erect a new consulate on the site at No. 6 Ōura. William Cowan submitted blueprints to the Office of Works in May 1905, proposing a two-story main building of brick construction with granite columns and appointments, tall domed towers on both sides, a roof of glazed tiles, detached kitchen, and small gardens circumscribed by a boundary wall. The plan included a two-story residence for British and Japanese staff on the site of the former stone warehouse at the rear of the property. Cowan provided an estimate of £5,700, hurrying to add that, "I have no reliable guide as to the cost of an entirely

---

[109] E. Hamilton Holmes (1876-1957) subsequently served at various posts in Korea and Japan until being promoted to consul at Shimonoseki in 1914 and going on to serve as consul-general at Yokohama from 1920 to 1936. He was a recipient of both the Silver Jubilee Medal and the Order of St Michael and St George for important non-military service overseas (Kuwata, p 310).

new building in Japan to enable me to do other than assume a cube price, but I will obtain tenders and submit a revised estimate thereon."[110]

Fig.4-3 William Cowan's original design for the Nagasaki British Consulate, submitted to the Office of Works in May 1905, featured twin towers at the front of the building. (UK National Archives)

Government architects at the Office of Works in London requested a number of alterations to reduce costs, such as the removal of dressing rooms at the rear of the main building, the construction of a flat rather than hipped roof, the reduction in width of the main indoor staircase, and the reuse of stone blocks from the old boundary wall. Cowan replied in August 1905, pointing out that:

> The accommodation, as provided, is demanded by the Minister, and I do not see that it can be reduced, as in my opinion it is all required. Something better than the ancient accommodation of forty years ago is now necessary, and the substantial modern buildings now erected for residences, public offices, etc. in Japan, are superior in design, and demand that a new British Consulate should be the same.[111]

Another motivation for the construction of a better grade of consulate in Nagasaki was the bond of British-Japanese friendship confirmed by the Anglo-Japanese Alliance of 1902 and tightened by cooperation between the two countries in the Russo-Japanese War. During a naval fete held in Nagasaki in November 1905 to celebrate the renewal of the alliance, Nagasaki Mayor Yokoyama Toraichirō commented as follows:

[110] William Cowan to the Office of Works, May 25, 1905 (WORK 10/359).
[111] William Cowan to the Principal Architect, Office of Works, August 18, 1905 (WORK 10/359).

Our two Island Empires, one the most powerful in the West and the other having just emerged victorious from a great conflict, are geographically widely separated from each other, but in heart and mind they are knit together as brothers. We feel that we owe a great deal to our Western brethren for the rapid development and improvement of our country. Moreover, the conclusion of the new treaty of alliance not only strengthens the intimate relations already existing between the two nations but ensures the peace of the Far East.[112]

Yokoyama's rosy assessment did not necessarily reflect the reality of British-Japanese relations in the wake of the Russo-Japanese War. On September 29, 1905, only days after the announcement of the terms of the Portsmouth Treaty, the British ambassador to Tokyo, C.M. Macdonald, sent a confidential circular to his consuls throughout Japan asking for lists of British subjects who could serve as interpreters in wartime. The timing and purport of the directive indicate that, however officially applauded, Japan's stunning victory in the Russo-Japanese War had sent chills down the British spine and invoked visions of an altercation between the two countries over conflicting interests in East Asia.

Harold G. Parlett, serving as acting consul during Frank W. Playfair's leave of absence, responded in January the following year with a list of only six people in the entire Nagasaki consular district—which included all of Nagasaki, Saga, Kumamoto and Kagoshima prefectures—thought to have a knowledge of Japanese sufficient to surmount the language barrier."[113] The document reveals the fact that most of the foreign residents of Nagasaki, even the sons of Frederick Ringer and other Britons who had been born and brought up there, had little competence in the language of their second homeland and continued to rely, as during the foreign settlement years, on Japanese staff for assistance in bridging the linguistic and cultural gap.

A Project Fraught with Trouble

William Cowan bent to the wishes of the government architects and scrapped both his original concept and a revised version. The official procrastination signaled the shift Britain's international relationships after the Russo-Japanese War and Nagasaki's sudden transformation from idyllic trade port to strategic naval station in the region. In 1906, Cowan submitted a new plan for the Nagasaki British Consulate that deleted the two domed towers at the front of the main building and much of the other ornamentation,

---

[112] *The Nagasaki Press,* November 9, 1905.
[113] Harold G. Parlett to Sir Claude MacDonald, January 8,1906 (FO 262/956).

NAGASAKI CONSULATE
WORKS-40/265

East Elevation

Front Elevation

Scale of feet

H.B.M.Office of Works
Shanghai, April 1906

Fig.4-4 William Cowan's revised design for the Nagasaki British Consulate, submitted in April 1906, was adopted by the Office of Works. (UK National Archives)

removed half of the second-story arches, and considerably scaled back the overall size of the buildings. He also acquiesced by reducing the width of the inner staircase and reusing stones from the old boundary wall. Cowan managed nevertheless to keep his hipped roof and to overrule the flat one, which had been recommended by the government architects but "would be difficult to keep watertight, and would tend to make the house most uncomfortably hot, the sun's heat on roofs is so excessive in summer, with the thermometre over 90° in the shade."[114]

The Office of Works invited tenders from local contractors and on August 11, 1906 reached an agreement with Nagasaki carpenter Gotō Kametarō for the construction of the new British consulate. The contract promised a payment of 50,000 yen in installments linked to the progress of the work and laid out more than 160 specifications regarding the style of the building and the materials to be used.[115] The two parties agreed on a period of eighteen months for the completion of the project. Most of the bricks, stone and lumber would be acquired locally, but other materials, such as porcelain basins and bathtubs, metal fittings and ornaments, were to be imported from abroad. Before erecting buildings, the contractor would have to drive piles into the soft earth on the lot, which had not been reinforced since its reclamation from the harbor in 1861. William Cowan appointed a clerk at the Office of Works in Shanghai to reside in Nagasaki and monitor the construction project.

The work did not proceed as expected. Cowan's representative, Cecil Simpson, visited Nagasaki in November and reported to the Office of Works that Gotō was bereft of funds and therefore borrowing money at "usurious rates of interest" before ordering materials, a situation that was seriously hindering the progress of the work. Another problem was a miscalculation in the extent of piling needed to support the new building: William Cowan had called for the use of logs eight-feet long and eight-inches in diameter, but the ground was so soft that these had to be increased to as much as eighteen feet long and ten inches in diameter. A total of 1,688 piles were required, causing a delay in the construction of the building and a sharp increase in the cost of materials.

Then in April the following year, Gotō vanished, bringing the work to a halt. When he reappeared, he blamed his absence on illness, but Cecil Simpson, deducing the real reason to be severe financial difficulties and trouble with lenders, convinced him to transfer the work to another contractor named Moritaka Ichidayū, who all along had been serving as co-contractor behind the scenes. Gotō and Moritaka signed a contract on June 24, 1907 agreeing that the latter would assume all "rights, privileges, liabilities and responsibilities" related to the construction of the new consulate. The

---

[114] The differing plans are preserved today at the National Archives of the UK, Kew (WORK 40/259-69).

[115] Nagasaki Prefecture Art Museum (ed.), *Nagasakishi eikokuryōjikan sekkei oyobi shiyōsho* (Design and Specifications of the British Consulate in Nagasaki City) (Nagasaki, 1990).

two men also acknowledged that the Office of Works would reimburse the contractor for expenditures beyond the scope of the original contract after the completion of the project.

Despite the promises laid out in the contract, Moritaka began to demand more money, citing factors such as the rising cost of materials and labor and the extra work requested by the Office of Works. Communication problems presented a further obstacle: "The native workmen on the job were self-opinionated and refused to carry out the Clerk of Works' instructions, leading to endless trouble. The contractor could not speak any English at all, not could our Clerk of Works speak any Japanese, and the interpreter was apparently afraid of the contractor."[116]

When the Office of Works insisted on the original terms of the contract, Moritaka threatened to remove fixtures from the building and sell them in the market. Cecil Simpson came to Nagasaki to reason with him, but the angry contractor only stepped up his demands, threatening to burn the building down or even commit suicide if the British did not add another 6,000 yen to the contract price. Frank W. Playfair asked the Nagasaki Prefecture Police for protection of British government property and wrote a private letter to the British ambassador in Tokyo, recommending that Moritaka's demands be met in order to avoid a costly legal battle and commenting that:

> The real reason for any trouble at all arises, in my opinion, from the fact of men of straw being given a contract of such magnitude. Before I went home [on leave of absence], I strongly impressed upon the late Surveyor Cowan the necessity of giving the contract to a Firm or Company of good standing, and not to any irresponsible individual who happened to put in the lowest tender. As a matter of fact this Moritaka is not a practical man at all and, I am informed, has often caused trouble and delay by interfering with his foreman, who is distinctly a capable workman (when sober!), and Goto— the original contractor—is little better than a carpenter, and had no capital. Though it seems rather a pity that we should give way, I really think that, under the circumstances, a compromise is desirable.[117]

Unexpectedly, the Nagasaki Prefecture Police persuaded Moritaka Ichidayū to terminate the contract in exchange for a severance payment of 3,000 yen, terms to which the Office of Works readily agreed. Moritaka removed his equipment from the site, and the Office of Works enlisted a team of day laborers to finish the work.

---

[116] Cecil Simpson to the Principal Architect, Office of Works, October 13, 1908 (WORK 10/359).
[117] F.W. Playfair to Sir Claude MacDonald, June 25, 1908 (FO 262/1007).

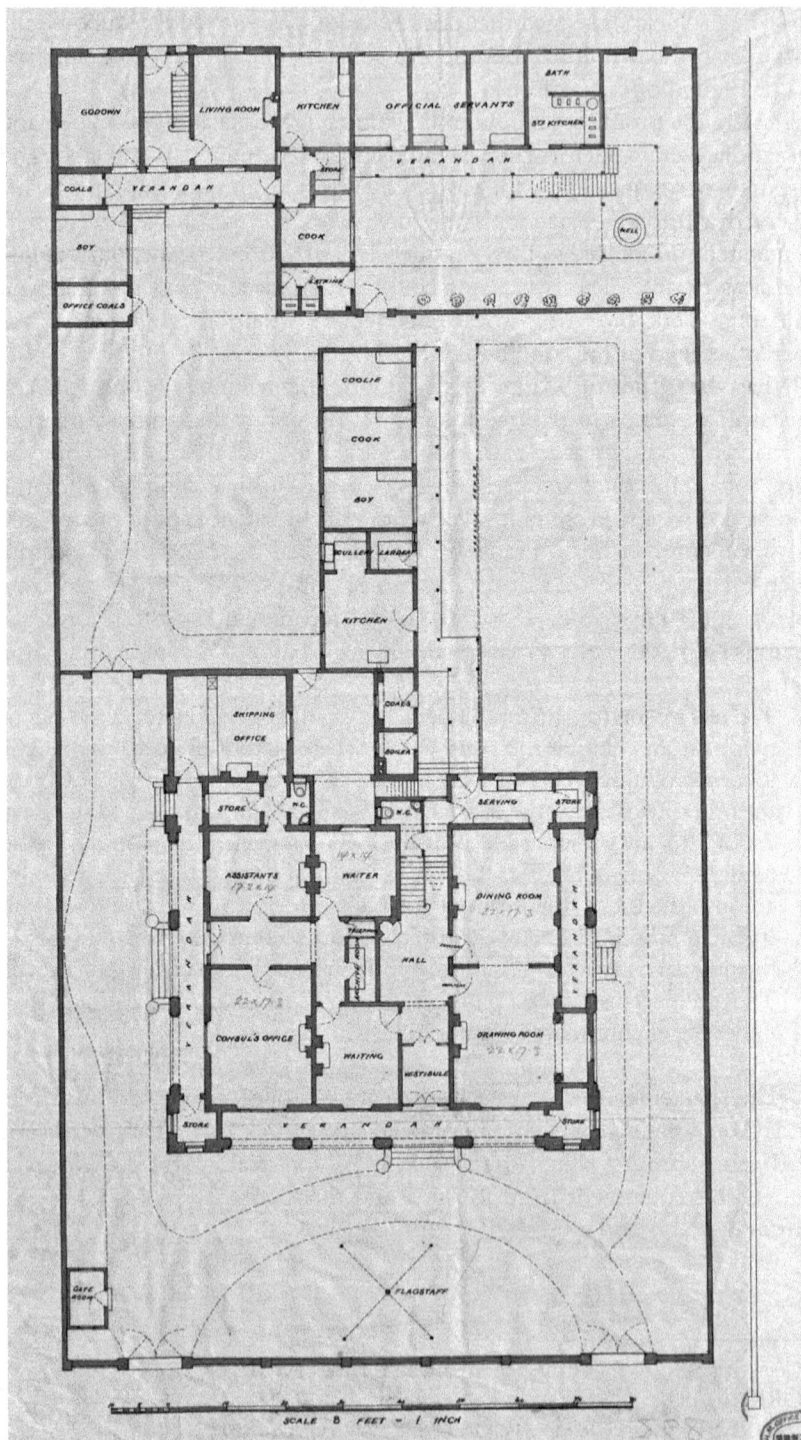

SCALE 8 FEET = 1 INCH

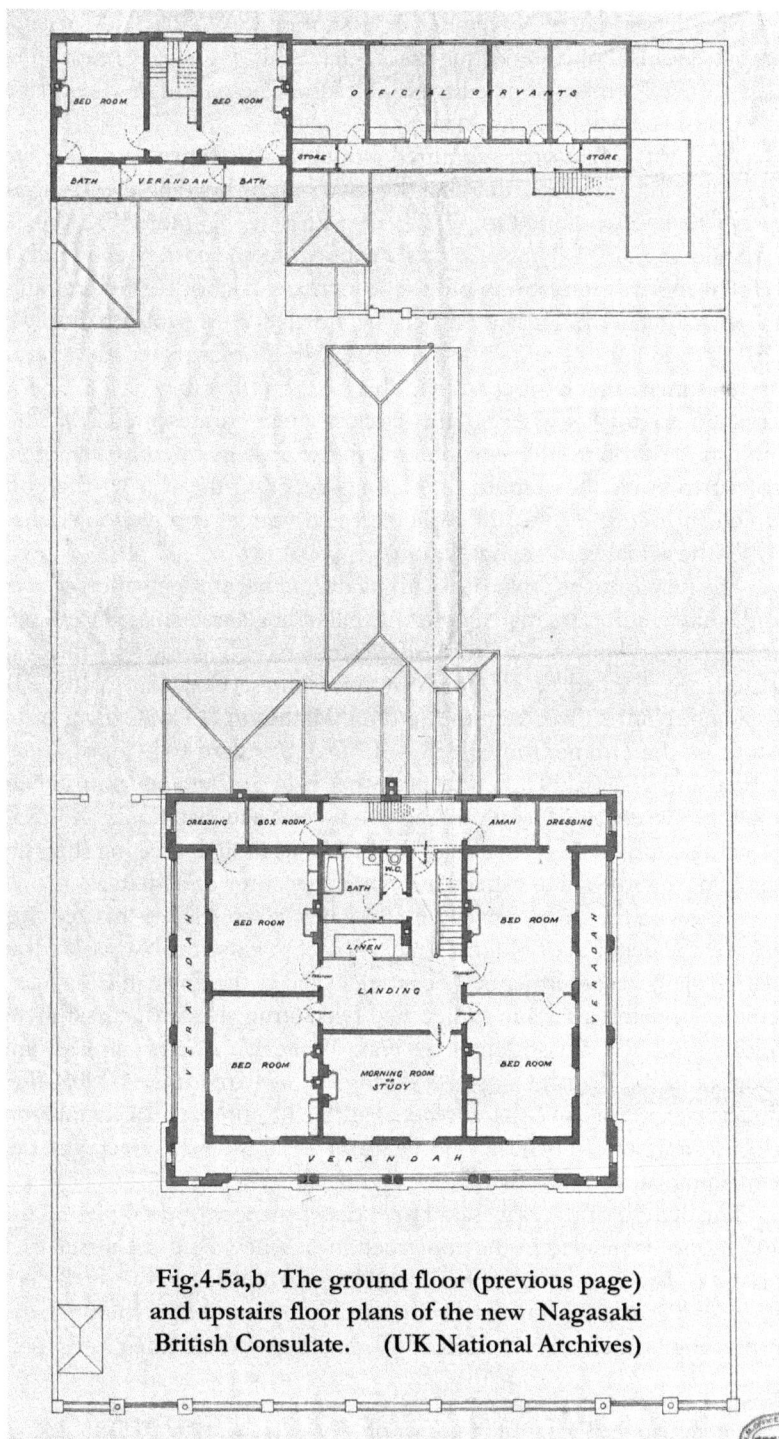

Fig.4-5a,b The ground floor (previous page) and upstairs floor plans of the new Nagasaki British Consulate.   (UK National Archives)

In a letter dated November 1, 108, Frank W. Playfair wrote to the ambassador in Tokyo reporting that, "I have this day taken occupation of the new Office Premises situated at No. 6 Ōura, where in future the business of the Consulate will be transacted."

The Office of Works submitted a final tally of expenses to the Treasury the following year, reporting that the total cost of building the new Nagasaki consulate had amounted to £7,270, or £1,570 (27%) more than the original estimate of £5,700. The spike was attributed to the cost of extra pilings and cement for the foundations and to the increase in labor costs stemming from the many delays. A Treasury official acknowledged the information with the terse comment: "I am to state that My Lords regret the very large underestimate that has occurred in this case, but that they give their covering sanction to the excesses in the circumstances represented."[118] The only indication of the trouble encountered in the process of construction was the cornerstone on the shipping clerk's residence at the rear of the complex, which showed the date 1907 (the expected year of completion) rather than 1908 (the actual year of completion).

The new British Consulate, with its distinctive amalgamation of red brick and white granite and matching front wall hiding a tree-shaded garden, added an elegant addition to the row of Western-style buildings on the Nagasaki waterfront, flanked to the north by the Chinese Consulate, Mitsui Bussan Building, Hunt's Pharmacy and Jardine, Matheson & Co. Office, and to the south by the Holme, Ringer & Co. Office, Standard Oil Co. of New York Office and Nagasaki Club. On the other side of Oura Creek, the Nagasaki Customs Matsugae Depot, Hong Kong & Shanghai Bank and Nagasaki Hotel also turned their facades to the harbor as though greeting ships arriving in the port and waiting expectantly for a new surge of activity.

However, the happy unveiling of the new consulate was marred the same year by the decision of Holme, Ringer & Co. to close the Nagasaki Hotel and sell off all its accouterments. The hotel, hailed as the finest in East Asia at the time of opening a decade earlier, had been struggling unsuccessfully to stay afloat since the Russo-Japanese War. While carpenters applied finishing touches to the British Consulate during the early months of 1908, the hotel directors, auditors and shareholders gathered to prepare for liquidation. The closure, announced officially on February 18, came into effect when the last remaining guest checked out after that date.

The demise of the Nagasaki Hotel cast a shadow of doubt on all the time and money expended in the construction of a new British Consulate. It was not an isolated event but rather the glaring symptom of an overall decline in the fortunes of Nagasaki as an international port. A large number of other hotels and businesses were similarly forced to pull down their signs as a result

---

[118] Treasury to the First Commissioner of Works, July 8, 1909 (WORK 10/359).

of the decrease in maritime traffic after the Russo-Japanese War.
One of the outcomes of the depression in Nagasaki's business activity
was an unprecedented exodus of Euro-American residents. The vacuum in
the harbor and in the shops and businesses of the town seemed to pull people
out of their houses on the Minamiyamate and Higashiyamate hillsides, down
the familiar stone-paved paths to the waterfront and into the cabins of
departing steamers, never to return. One of the foreigners participating in the
emigration in 1908 was Robert N. Walker, a British former ship captain who
had founded a successful shipchandling business in Nagasaki during the
boom years around the turn of the century.

The author of an article entitled *The Decline of Nagasaki* in an English-
language newspaper in Kobe commented on the trend as follows:

> The next few weeks will witness the departure of no fewer than 35 foreign
> residents of Nagasaki. Of these not more than eleven are going on furlough,
> so that none of the others are expected to return. Two of the best-known of
> those that are leaving for good are Mr. John H. Shaw and Mr. Clark, who have
> just severed their long connection with the Mitsu Bishi Shipbuilding Yards.
> Considering the recent advances that have been made there under their
> supervision it is not easy to see how their services can be dispensed with; but
> this is probably one more indication of the movement in Japan towards doing
> without the assistance of foreign experts in modern industries... Mr. R.N.
> Walker, who has been for many years a prominent businessman of Nagasaki,
> is also moving with his family to Vancouver, B.C.[119]

The author goes on to blame the decline on Nagasaki Customs officials
who insist on opening and inspecting all the luggage of passengers in transit
and thus discourage people from landing. But of course the reasons for
Nagasaki's troubles in 1908 ran deeper than irritations at the waterfront.
During the first decades after the opening of Japan's doors, Nagasaki had not
only been the closest Japanese port to China but also the only place in the
country with an infrastructure geared to foreign trade. Then the increased
European military and colonial presence in East Asia at the end of the
nineteenth century and the sharp increase in international shipping and
tourism had brought a few golden years of prosperity to the port as a secure
harbor and coaling station.

But things had changed. The revision of Japan's international treaties in
1899 had allowed Moji, Karatsu, Kuchinotsu and other small domestic ports
in western Japan to open their doors to international trade and thus to share
in the wealth monopolized previously by Nagasaki. The Russo-Japanese War
and the enforcement of martial law had given the other cities a head start by
halting international trade in Nagasaki and delaying the Nagasaki harbor

---

[119] *The Japan Weekly Chronicle*, March 19, 1908.

improvement project. Moreover, the import of steel for shipbuilding and railways, which had been one of the pillars of trade in Nagasaki, had declined because Japanese steel mills in northern Kyushu were answering a considerable portion of the demand and had little or no need to rely on the services of foreign importers, brokers or insurers. The Mitsubishi Nagasaki Shipyard and Engine Works was Nagasaki's one shining star, but, as the author of the above article mentions, it was replacing foreign experts with graduates from Japanese universities and depending less on the help of the foreign community. The fact that the tonnage of domestically built ships surpassed that of imported ships for the first time in 1908 tells everything about the mood of Japan and Nagasaki the year that British residents Robert N. Walker, John H. Shaw and James Clark pull up stakes—and, ironically, the new Nagasaki British Consulate opened its doors.[120]

---

[120] Nagasaki City Chronology, p 142.

5 SUNSET IN NAGASAKI

FRANK W. PLAYFAIR retired from the Japan Consular Service in October 1909, less than a year after supervising the move to the new consulate, and left Nagasaki amid expressions of thanks from friends and colleagues.[121] A series of experienced consuls and acting consuls filled his shoes over the following years, including Arthur M. Chalmers (1909-1912), Ralph G. Forster (1912-1913) and John B. Rentiers (1914-1915). The consulate at No. 6 Ōura meanwhile settled into the row of waterfront buildings, serving as the face of Nagasaki greeting people arriving by ship, a safe haven and information center for British residents, and a venue for meetings, wedding receptions, and parties for Japanese guests.

Visitors entered the compound through one of the two front gates and climbed a short flight of steps to the front door of the main building. To the right of the entrance vestibule was the public area comprised of a large parlor and dining room with high ceilings and windows; to the left was the administrative section including a waiting room, the consul's office, storage space and closets for archives, stationery and utensils. Each of the large rooms featured an English-style coal-burning fireplace with a decorative wooden mantel and iron canopy. The consul and his family lived in the second floor rooms of the main building, including four bedrooms and a study, bathroom and antechambers. Out the back door was a long single-story building with a boiler room, coal shed, kitchen and servants' quarters flanked by gardens. The two-story building at the rear of the property was separated into two parts: one a Western-style brick structure that served as living space for the shipping clerk; the other a wooden building with rows of tatami-matted compartments and other facilities for Japanese employees and their families.

---

[121] Kuwata, pp 424-5. Playfair died in Edinburgh in 1915.

Fig.5-1a,b (Above) The Nagasaki British Consulate seen from the front in a photograph taken in 1911, three years after the completion of the new buildings. (Below) The buildings on the left and right, seen across the inner garden, are the shipping clerk's quarters and a dormitory for Japanese employees, respectively. (UK National Archives)

As feared, the grand consulate buildings never justified the optimism surrounding their construction. Nagasaki failed to regain its status as an international port after the Russo-Japanese War of 1904-5, which had fostered British-Japanese cooperation but exerted a largely negative effect on the port by evoking martial law, restricting harbor traffic, and allowing other ports in western Japan to enter the forum of trade previously monopolized by Nagasaki. The intervening years had seen a sharp decline in the foreign population of the city and a commensurate drain on trade and cultural exchange.

However temporary, the outbreak of World War One in the summer of 1914 brought a flurry of activity to Nagasaki and strengthened Anglo-Japanese ties in the port. When the German colony of Tsingtao (Qingdao) fell to a joint Japanese and British force in November, the citizens of Nagasaki participated by the thousands in a mass celebration at Suwa Shinto Shrine and a lantern parade that snaked through the city to the front of the British Consulate. The following month, George P. Paton (first assistant acting as consul in the absence of John B. Rentiers) hosted a reception at the British consulate for a group of officers involved in the seizure of Tsingtao, his felicitations revealing the unity of Britain and Japan in efforts to subjugate a mutual enemy.[122]

Fig.5-2 The Ōura Bund (waterfront) captured in a picture postcard circa 1920. The buildings (from right to left) are the Holme, Ringer & Co. office and the British Consulate. (Private collection)

---

[122] *The Nagasaki Press*, December 29, 1914.

British residents of Nagasaki, although steadily declining in number, came together to support the war effort and form local branches of the Patriotic League of Britons Overseas and the British Ladies Patriotic League. Various events were held to raise funds, including the Garden Fete held in May every year from 1916 to 1918 in the Ringer residence at No. 14 Minamiyamate. The long reports published by *The Nagasaki Press* each year read like a roll call of foreign residents of Nagasaki and a testimony to Anglo-Japanese cooperation during World War One. The participants collected money from ticket sales, stalls selling refreshments and crafts, and a concert arranged by volunteers from both the foreign and Japanese community. "Young ladies and children sold sweets, flags, programmes, fans, etc.," reported the newspaper in May 1916, "and were conspicuous by reason of charming dresses, reluctance to give change, and inability to remember faces. Their efforts resulted in substantial additions to the receipts."[123]

John B. Rentiers moved to Manila in January 1915, and John T. Wawn arrived from Chemulpo (Incheon) to take over as British consul at Nagasaki. Wawn had entered the Japan Consular Service as a nineteen-year-old student interpreter in 1896, running the usual gauntlet of positions in Japan, China, Formosa and Korea before his promotion to consul and appointment to Nagasaki. However, it was to be his last. Suffering from alcoholism and fatigue, the forty-one year-old retired from the Japan Consular Service in April 1918 and retired to the countryside near Nagasaki. His successor was Thomas J. Harrington, consul at Tamsui, Formosa (Taiwan) for the previous five years.

The Armistice of November 1918 occasioned celebrations as enthusiastic in Nagasaki as in other Allied cities around the world. But far from ushering in a new era of prosperity, the end of the conflict dragged Japan into a recession. The enormous expenditures of the war meanwhile threw Britain into debt, doubled inflation over a period of about six years, and reduced the value of the Pound Sterling by more than 60%. The British government responded to the crisis by slashing expenses and jettisoning property throughout the Empire. The Foreign Office reduced its diplomatic presence in Japan, closing consulates in Shimonoseki, Hakodate and other ports and transferring duties to consular agents. Another unexpected outcome of the war was an increased sense of autonomy in Commonwealth countries like Canada, New Zealand and India that had bravely supported the war effort. For various reasons, Japan also began to drift away from its old friend, psychologically as well as politically.

---

[123] *The Nagasaki Press*, 23 May 1916.

The Last Shipping Clerk

George Kircher was appointed shipping clerk in Nagasaki in the wake of the treaty revisions of 1899 and the elimination of the position of constable by British authorities. He retired in November 1902 and gave the reins to Percy C. Vincent, formerly an employee of Holme, Ringer & Co. The duties of shipping clerk became heavier after Japan's victory in the Russo-Japanese War and the resumption of visits to Nagasaki by foreign warships, merchantmen and passenger liners, overtaxing an already frail Percy C. Vincent. The forty-three-year-old suffered a severe stroke in the middle of a naval court of inquiry held at the consulate on December 19, 1905 and expired three days later, leaving a Japanese widow and two children. Harold G. Parlett, serving as acting consul during Frank W. Playfair's leave of absence, reported the tragedy to Tokyo, commenting that, "I have always considered it regrettable that the services of a man in so poor a state of health as Mr. Vincent was ever secured for the office. At the same time, so small are the inducements of the post he occupied that a Consul can have but little choice of candidates. I have much pleasure, however, in testifying to Mr. Vincent's zeal in endeavoring to do his work properly."[124]

In a follow-up dated December 27, Parlett informs the ambassador that he had hired a young man named James S. Waddell to fill the post of shipping clerk. The twenty-two-year-old native of Stirling, Scotland had arrived in Nagasaki a few weeks earlier as third mate on the British steamship *Dumbarton* and had appeared at the consulate with a letter of recommendation from his captain. Parlett engaged Waddell on the condition that he acknowledge "that by accepting the post of shipping clerk here, he is throwing away his opportunities in his own profession, as no hope can be held out to him of any increase in his salary or yet of promotion." The young Briton's eagerness to accept the post despite its rather dreary prospects suggests that he had found another important motivation to stay in Nagasaki, perhaps the attractions of the Japanese woman whom he would later marry.[125] Waddell proved his abilities so well that in 1911 he was offered a transfer—along with the raise in salary predicted impossible by Parlett—to the British consulate-general in Kobe where he would remain in charge of the shipping department until the eve of World War Two.

Waddell's successor in Nagasaki was John A. Marston, a former soldier in the Royal Welsh Fusiliers who assumed the post of shipping clerk on February 1, 1911 at a salary of 125 yen per month. Marston had already been

---

[124] Harold G. Parlett to Sir Claude MacDonald, December 22, 1905 (FO 262/937).
[125] James S. Waddell married Okawauchi Kane, a native of Imari, Saga Prefecture, in a ceremony at the British consulate in August 1909.

Fig.5-3 John A. Marston and his son Jack pose for a photograph in Nagasaki around the time of the former's employment as shipping clerk at the British Consulate. (Courtesy of Joy Rush)

residing in Nagasaki for several years. His name first appears in local records in March 1906, when his Japanese wife Chie gave birth to a son while staying at the Hotel de France. After a three-year blank, he appears again in the 1909 issue of the *Japan Directory* as editor of the English-language newspaper *The Nagasaki Press* and, the following year, as an English instructor at the Nagasaki Commercial School. A Freemason, Marston had been initiated into the Nagasaki Masonic Lodge on the same day as James S. Waddell (February 4, 1910), suggesting that the two men were friends and that the latter had recommended him for the job of shipping clerk.

In 1914, John A. Marston transferred to the British consulate in

Shimonoseki.[126] David Waddell, brother of James S. Waddell, took his place in Nagasaki and moved into the Western-style quarters at the rear of the consulate with his wife and two children, who had come out from Britain to join him. Despite the paltry compensation, Waddell excelled at his job, as evidenced by John T. Wawn's comment in his last letter as Nagasaki consul in March 1918 that "the work of Mr. Waddell has been of the greatest use: in fact, it is no exaggeration to say, that, had it not been for his most loyal and willing help, I could not have carried on the work of the Consulate until to-day, in view of my present uncertain state of health."[127]

Wawn's successor Robert Boulter also stood behind David Waddell. He suggested that, like the members of the Japan Consular Service, Waddell should receive a 20% increase in wages to cope with the sharp hike in the cost of living after World War One. In a long letter to the British ambassador in August 1918, Boulter points out that the living expenses of the Waddell family had increased from 118 yen in 1915 to 189 yen in 1918 and that the shipping clerk's monthly salary of 130 yen, even when supplemented by incidental income from clerical services, was simply not enough for a "European family" to make ends meet in Japan.[128] He does not mention his own salary, a spectacular 750 yen plus bonuses and living expenses.

The significance of 130 yen per month—and the continuing economic disparity between Westerners and Japanese—is underlined by the information given by Boulter in an earlier letter asking for an increase in wages for Japanese employees.[129] The list of occupations and wages provided by the acting consul shows that the highest monthly salary was the forty yen paid to Nakao Tanekichi, a writer and translator who had been in the employ of the consulate since 1876. The lowest was the meager fifteen yen per month paid to the watchman.

David Waddell's wife Minnie gave birth to a third child on December 23, 1918, a daughter named Winifred who was the first and, as it would turn out, only child to be born in the consular premises at No. 6 Ōura. In April 1920, Waddell accepted a transfer to the British consulate-general in Yokohama and left Nagasaki with his family, never to return. After his departure, the Foreign Office decided to dispense with the post of shipping clerk in Nagasaki and to entrust the related duties to a Japanese employee.

---

[126] John A. Marston resigned in July 1918 and returned to Nagasaki to resume work at *The Nagasaki Press*, but poor health forced him to retire at the end of the following year. He moved with his family to Kobe and secured employment at the Far Eastern Advertising Company, but his health continued to deteriorate. He returned to England in May 1922 to convalesce but died in November the same year, leaving his Japanese widow and two children in Kobe.

[127] John T. Wawn to Sir W. Conyngham Greene, March 31, 1918 (FO 262/1351).

[128] Robert Boulter to Sir W. Conyngham Greene, August 12, 1918 (FO 262/1351).

[129] Robert Boulter to Sir W. Conyngham Greene, June 4, 1918 (FO 262/1351).

Anglo-Japanese Alliance, Cancelled

Oswald White arrived in Nagasaki in January 1920 and took over for Thomas J. Harrington, who proceeded to Manila to assume the post of consul-general of the Philippines. Before leaving Nagasaki, Harrington enlisted Jewish auctioneer Sigmund Lessner to conduct a public sale of his personal belongings in the consular premises at No. 6 Ōura. The notice carried in *The Nagasaki Press* provides a list of the items to be sold, everything from silver candelabra to mirrored dressing tables, fine carved wood sideboards, revolving bookcases, carpets, curtains and a "good piano by C. Rordorf & Co., Zurich." The notice indicates that the members of the Japan Consular Service were responsible for furnishing their own quarters and that they had to haul a considerable amount of furniture and other belongings from one post to another. It also suggests that Thomas J. Harrington, perhaps because of the transfer to faraway Manila, decided to reduce his luggage expenses.

Oswald White had passed the competitive examination to the Japan Consular Service in 1903 at the age of twenty and served in a number of positions in Japan and Korea before his promotion to consul at Tamsui, Formosa in 1919. He arrived in Nagasaki amid cold weather and a lingering influenza epidemic and moved into the upstairs rooms of the main consulate building at No. 6 Ōura with his wife Kathleen and three daughters. Kathleen had spent several years in Nagasaki as a child while her father, the illustrious John C. Hall, was serving as acting consul in the port.

During Oswald White's four-year stint as consul, a number of events on the world stage accelerated Nagasaki's decline as an international port and reduced the usefulness of the British consulate. In November 1921, President Warren G. Harding convened the Washington Naval Conference in the American capital and asked Japan, Britain and several other leading countries to send delegations to discuss military and territorial issues related to the Asia-Pacific Region. Two of the international agreements that resulted from the conference affected Nagasaki, namely the Four-Power Treaty and the Five-Power Treaty, the latter better known as the "Washington Naval Treaty." The former called on Britain, the United States, Japan and France to refrain from further territorial expansion in the region and to terminate the Anglo-Japanese Alliance, up for renewal but increasingly criticized, particularly by the United States, as exclusive and out of synchrony with conditions after World War One. The latter meanwhile required Britain, the United States, Japan, France and Italy to limit the construction of warships.

Fig.5-4a,b Oswald White served as Nagasaki British Consul from 1920 to 1925. (Below) His daughters, dressed in their father's clothes, play in the garden behind the consulate building at No. 6 Ōura. (Private collection)

On December 17, 1921, only five days after the signing of the Four-Power Treaty, Oswald White attended the launching ceremony of the 40,000-ton battleship *Tosa* at the Mitsubishi Nagasaki Shipyard. Some 50,000 spectators gathered on the waterfront and surrounding hillsides, and two seaplanes from the Naval Aviation Corps in Sasebo circled the harbor during the ceremony, "giving the inhabitants of the city by far the best aviation display ever seen at Nagasaki and creating considerable unrest among sea-birds."[130] The mood of the participants, however, was anything but jubilant because of the already widely recognized likelihood that the *Tosa* would be scrapped according to the terms of the Washington Naval Treaty. An event at the launching ceremony presaged the sad fate of the ship: the ceremonial *kusudama* (a piñata-like ball filled with confetti and streamers) failed to break open and release its contents. Sure enough, the treaty signed on February 6, 1922 tagged the *Tosa* for destruction. Still unfitted, the warship was towed to the coast of Tosa, the town in Shikoku Island from which it took its name, and used for artillery practice until it finally sank.

Around the same time, news of the impending visit of the Prince of Wales (the future Edward VIII) sent a wave of excitement through the British community of Japan but caused only disappointment in Nagasaki because the port was not on the prince's itinerary.[131] Oswald White joined the Ringer brothers and other British residents in petitioning the embassy in Tokyo for a royal visit, but his efforts were futile: the prince bypassed Nagasaki and called instead at Kagoshima on the same island of Kyushu, a snub that aggravated awareness of Nagasaki's fading profile in commercial and cultural exchanges between Britain and Japan.

The limitations imposed by the Washington Naval Treaty meanwhile exerted a devastating effect on the Nagasaki economy. With both foreign trade and fisheries declining rapidly and the cost of living soaring after World War One, the Mitsubishi Nagasaki Shipyard and affiliated factories remained as the last pillars of local industry, but the cancelation of naval contracts caused the number of employees to plummet from 18,008 in 1921 to only 7,716 in 1925.[132]

Oswald White and family left Nagasaki and returned to England on a nine-month furlough in February 1923, leaving the consulate in the hands of a young diplomat named Reginald McPherson Austin. The timing allowed Austin to celebrate the inauguration of the Japan-China Rapid Express

---

[130] *The Nagasaki Press*, December 20, 1921.

[131] *The Nagasaki Press*, March 11, 1922.

[132] Nishi-Nippon Jūkōgyō Kabushikaisha Nagasaki Zōsenjo (ed.), *Mitsubishi nagasaki zōsenjoshi zokuhen* (Nagasaki, 1951), p. 38. The number decreased to a low of 6,127 in 1932—the lowest point in Nagasaki's post World War One depression—and then climbed back to a high of 25,013 in 1941 during the construction of the battleship *Musashi*. (Ibid, p. 66)

Service in May 1923, a twice-weekly commute using two state-of-the-art steamships built for Nippon Yusen Kaisha (NYK) on the River Clyde in Glasgow. He could also enjoy a pleasant summer holiday in the hill resort of Unzen near Nagasaki, increasingly popular among the expatriate residents of Shanghai, Hong Kong and Vladivostok. But after the Great Kanto Earthquake of September 1, 1923, a catastrophe that destroyed vast swatches of Tokyo and Yokohama, it fell on his shoulders to orchestrate the British response in Nagasaki and to call on foreign residents for assistance to refugees.

One of the more than 140,000 people to perish in the earthquake was David Waddell, who had left Nagasaki for Yokohama three years earlier. Although appointed to the position of clerk at the British Embassy, Waddell had been unfortunate enough to be visiting the Yokohama Consulate-General when the buildings collapsed in the earthquake.[133] His remains were later buried in the foreign cemetery at Yokohama. Minnie Waddell and her now four children survived and escaped the disaster area on a steamship to Kobe, and they returned heartbroken to Scotland the following year.

When Oswald White resumed his post in November, Nagasaki had reverted to its former peaceful if economically stagnant situation. The *Nagasaki-maru* and *Shanghai-maru*, appropriated to assist in the emergency transportation of refugees, were back in operation on the Japan-China Rapid Express Service, but the Mitsubishi Nagasaki Shipyard and other industrial facilities in the city were still dithering in the midst of recession. As de facto head of the local European community, White officiated at various social gatherings and maintained close ties with business leaders and government officials. In December 1923, he presided over discussions regarding the sale of the Public Hall, which had served for decades as a venue for meetings, concerts, magic shows and various other events in the foreign settlement but now was haunted by ghosts of a bygone era. With White serving as trustee, the old building was sold to a Japanese Protestant Church, torn down, and replaced with a wooden church building.[134] In May the following year, White's position of prominence in the local community was reaffirmed by his election as vice-president of the Nagasaki International Club, a gentlemen's organization established in 1899 to promote friendship and cooperation among leading Japanese and foreign residents.

---

[133] *The Japan Weekly Chronicle*, October 4, 1923.
[134] At the time of this writing, the church is still standing on the site of the former Public Hall at No. 31 Oura, beside the Confucian Shrine in the former Nagasaki Foreign Settlement.

16 British Consulate at Nagasaki. 長崎大浦英國領事館

Fig.5-5a,b Picture postcards show (above) the *Nagasaki-maru* anchored at Dejima Wharf circa 1925 and (below) the Nagasaki British Consulate and Holme, Ringer & Co. office at No. 6 and No. 7 Ōura. The boat used by the consul to row out to ships visiting Nagasaki is hanging from davits on the far right. The waterfront street is still a narrow thoroughfare providing a wide-open view over the harbor. (Private collection)

It was probably with a sense of relief that Oswald White moved on to a new appointment as consul in Dairen, China in April 1925.[135] His successor in Nagasaki was Montague B.T. Paske-Smith, a member of the Japan Consular Service since 1907. Early in his career, Paske-Smith had spent several years in the Philippine capital of Manila where he learned Spanish and married Maria Teresa Bertran de Lis, a native of Madrid. Promoted from the post of vice-consul at Kobe, he arrived in Nagasaki with his wife and two daughters and took up residence in the consular premises at No. 6 Ōura. The family found a port steeped in history and natural beauty but exuding little of its former color and activity. The Nagasaki Hotel, Belle Vue Hotel, Cliff House and other iconic hotels of the foreign settlement period had closed and the buildings passed into Japanese hands. Meanwhile, fewer foreign merchantmen and passenger liners than ever were calling at the port, even to take on the bunker coal so prized at the end of the previous century. In 1925, only ninety-four foreign merchantmen entered Nagasaki Harbor, less than 13% of the peak figure of 726 ships recorded in 1898.[136]

The free time in Nagasaki allowed Paske-Smith to devote himself to research on local history. Like many of his colleagues and predecessors, he engaged in scholarly studies and contributed to the field of Japanology, but he was unusual in that he focused, not on Japanese culture or politics *per se* but on the history of Christianity and the activities of foreigners. One of his best-known works is *Western Barbarians in Japan and Formosa in Tokugawa Days, 1603-1868*, a ground-breaking study that laid the foundation for future research on the foreign settlements of Meiji-period Japan. As acting consul for the Netherlands, he also arranged for the restoration of the Dutch Cemetery at Goshinji, a Buddhist temple in the Inasa neighborhood of Nagasaki. Established in 1654, the cemetery had been used over the centuries by the employees of the Dutch Factory on Dejima but had fallen into disrepair after the last burial in 1870.

Montague B.T. Paske-Smith left Nagasaki in December 1927 and filled a number of posts in Japan, China and the Philippines before taking charge of the British consulate in Honolulu, Hawaii in 1932. In 1934, he left the Japan Consular Service to work in Spain and two years later received the illustrious appointment of envoy extraordinary and minister plenipotentiary to Bogota, Colombia. He received the Order of St Michael and St George for important service overseas in 1941 and died in London in 1946.

---

[135] Oswald White went on to serve as consul-general at Seoul and Mukden until the eve of World War Two, when he returned to England. He was a recipient of both the Silver Jubilee Medal and the Order of St Michael and St George for important non-military service overseas. (Kuwata, p 478)

[136] Nagasaki City Chronology, p 133 and 161.

Paske-Smith's beautiful elder daughter Maria Teresa ("Chiquita") Paske-Smith y Bertran de Lis, born in 1913 to Paske-Smith and his Spanish wife, married the American band leader Eddy Duchin and was immortalized in the 1956 Hollywood movie *The Eddy Duchin Story*. His second daughter Isabel, born in the Philippines in 1916, married George Millar, a renowned journalist, soldier and World War Two resistance leader in France who wrote a book in her honor entitled *Isabel and the Sea* (1948).[137]

Fig.5-6 Maria Teresa ("Chiquita"), the elder daughter of Nagasaki British Consul Montague B.T. Paske-Smith. (Private collection)

---

[137] http://www.independent.co.uk/news/obituaries/george-millar-6149727.html

6 THE LAST CONSUL

WHEN FERDINAND C. GREATREX took over for Montague B.T. Paske-Smith in December 1927, he probably never imagined that he would remain at the post of British consul in Nagasaki longer than any of his predecessors or, even less, that he would be the last in the long line of British consuls dating back to the opening of Japan's doors in 1859.

Born in London in 1884, Greatrex had passed the competitive examination to the Japan Consular Service in 1906 at the young age of eighteen. He rose through the ranks over the following years, starting as a student interpreter in Tokyo and serving as an assistant and vice-consul in various ports. He married Alys Cahusac in Tokyo in 1912 and had two sons, both born in Japan. As acting consul in Shimonoseki, he oversaw the closure of the British consulate in that port in 1922 and the transfer of diplomatic duties to a consular agent. His next posting was Hakodate, where again the duty of downgrading the consulate to a branch of the Yokohama British Consulate fell on his shoulders. Although scheduled to assume the position of consul at Tamsui, Formosa (Taiwan), he was appointed instead to Nagasaki in late 1927. His sister Muriel was married to the British conductor Sir Henry Wood, who had an indirect connection with Nagasaki in that he had discovered Miura Tamaki, the prima donna who won international fame for her portrayal of Cho-Cho-san in the Puccini opera *Madama Butterfly*.

Ferdinand C. Greatrex arrived in Nagasaki without his family. His wife had remained in England with their sons, not out of reluctance to live in Japan, but because of her husband's infidelity and the ensuing breakdown of their marriage. Greatrex's only companions were Konishi Kizō and his wife, natives of Shiga Prefecture who had been serving the consul as a cook and housekeeper for several years. He took up lodgings in one of the second-floor bedrooms of the main building at No. 6 Ōura, sat at the desk in the

Fig.6-1 Ferdinand C. Greatrex as a young diplomat in Japan.
(Courtesy of Andrew Greatrex)

consul's office assisted solely by a Japanese clerk, and ate alone at the huge dinner table in the consulate dining room.

Greatrex had barely unpacked his suitcases when *The Nagasaki Press*, the last English-language newspaper in this port, ceased publication. From the time that *The Nagasaki Shipping List and Advertiser* made its mark in 1861 as Japan's first modern newspaper and the official mouthpiece of the British Legation in Edo, the English-language newspapers of Nagasaki had served as a vehicle of communication for foreign residents while at the same time providing the world with a window on events at the western edge of the archipelago. The editor of the Kobe newspaper *The Japan Chronicle* devoted space in his columns to the subject, calling *The Nagasaki Press* "the oldest foreign newspaper in Japan" and reporting on its demise as follows:

> For several years past such an ending seemed inevitable; in fact from the time of the Russo-Japanese War, when the trade of the port sustained a

severe blow by the stoppage of the lucrative trade with North China and Siberia. When the war ended the business, or the greater part of it, went to the newer ports of Moji and Tsuruga. In course of time the trade would have gone to those ports, as they are better situated for its conduct, but the war provided an opportunity for summary transfer which would otherwise have been lacking. The great improvement in means of communication also gravely affected the *Press*, as much larger journals published at Shanghai and Kobe reached Nagasaki in twenty-four hours with world news in greater detail than could possibly be supplied by the local paper. Another factor, possibly, was the lack of support from the foreign community, which is small and transient, few residents expecting to make a permanent stay in the port and fewer still being interested in its business prosperity.[138]

Nagasaki's prospects became even dimmer when the world stumbled through the Great Depression at the end of the decade and Japan began to clash with the international community over its actions in Manchuria. In the autumn of 1931, the British Foreign Office aired a proposal to close the Nagasaki consulate and sell the property at No. 6 Ōura. In a letter from Tokyo dated October 14, 1931, British Ambassador Sir Francis O. Lindley informed Ferdinand C. Greatrex that he had been asked by the Foreign Office to submit his views on the abolition of the consulate because "it is the feeling of the Foreign Office that there is not actually sufficient work at Nagasaki to require the presence of a salaried officer."[139]

Greatrex responded on October 18 and 29 with long letters outlining the situation in the Nagasaki district, which included all of Kyushu and the areas formerly under the jurisdiction of the Shimonoseki consulate. According to Greatrex, the consulate was earning enough revenue from bills of clearance and other administrative services to meet its expenses, the decrease in receipts at Nagasaki in recent years being offset by a commensurate increase at Shimonoseki. He pointed out that the market for real estate in Nagasaki was extremely depressed and that the sale of the consular buildings could not be expected to fetch any significant sum, and he predicted that, in any case, "all classes of Japanese set great store by the historical associations of this place with foreign countries, and the first suggestion of our withdrawal will, I am sure, cause a much greater outcry than that heard in the case of Hakodate or Shimonoseki."

Greatrex went on to report that the consulate, now staffed solely by the consul and a low-paid Japanese clerk, was handling a large number of tasks aside from services to visiting British ships, including liaison with Japanese officials and British residents (the latter numbering about 130, exclusive of

---

138 *The Japan Chronicle*, August 8, 1928.
139 Sir F.O Lindley to F.C. Greatrex, October 14, 1931, in a folder entitled "Nagasaki Consulate Proposed Closing Down" (FO 796/192).

summertime visitors to the nearby resort of Unzen), the issuing of passports to Britons and visas to Japanese travelers, correspondence with the British Embassy and the consular agent in Shimonoseki, and clerical work related to commercial inquiries, the administration of estates, and disbursements to British government pensioners living in the district.

The table of revenue and expenditures submitted by Greatrex shows that the average annual revenue from fees (1922-1931) was about 16,000 yen and the average yearly expenses during the same period 12,000 yen, leaving a balance of 4,000 yen. The expenses included the remuneration paid to the consular agent in Shimonoseki, the salaries of the Japanese clerk and servants, and expenditures arising from the upkeep of the consulate and the purchase of stationery and supplies. The table did not, however, include the emoluments paid to the consul, who was a senior officer in the Japan Consular Service and demanded a fitting stipend. In a memorandum on the subject, the Foreign Office estimated that the money paid to the consul averaged (where one pound sterling was equivalent to ten yen) about 14,600 yen per annum, including the consul's salary (9,000 yen), local allowance (1,000 yen), representation allowance (2,500 yen), and cost of living bonus (2,100 yen).

One suggestion raised in the course of discussions was to employ former Nagasaki consul John T. Wawn—who had retired in 1918 but remained in the Nagasaki area—as an unpaid acting consul, allowing him to reside rent-free in the consulate. Greatrex supported the idea, adding in one of his letters that, although Wawn had become somewhat of a recluse, "I believe he is completely cured of his dipsomania [i.e. alcoholism] and I have gathered from his conversation that he often contemplates the possible advantages of a more active and sociable life."

John T. Wawn apparently turned down the offer of work as a consular agent. As an alternative, the Foreign Office suggested the appointment of Frederick E.E. (Freddy) Ringer and his younger brother Sydney A. Ringer as consular agents because they were natives of Nagasaki, leading British residents in the port and already jointly held the position of honorary vice-consul. In the end, however, the Foreign Office decided to maintain the status quo in Nagasaki and Shimonoseki. The Nagasaki British Consulate continued to function, and Ferdinand C. Greatrex kept his jurisdiction over British interests in the entire region including the port of Shimonoseki, the area of northern Fukuoka Prefecture encompassing the prefecture capital of Fukuoka, the trade port of Moji, and the city of Kokura gaining clout as a steel-manufacturing center.

Holme, Ringer & Company

Soon after the Meiji Restoration of 1868, British merchants Edward Z. Holme and Frederick Ringer took over the tea business conducted to date by Glover & Co. and founded Holme, Ringer & Co. in an office in the Nagasaki Foreign Settlement. Holme later returned to England, but Ringer remained in Nagasaki and expanded operations and served as local agent for dozens of foreign insurance, shipping and banking firms. The company opened a branch office in Shimonoseki in 1890, skirting the restriction on business activities outside the treaty ports by calling it Wuriu Shokwai and placing a Japanese businessman in charge. The company also established branch offices in Korea and Russia. International trade declined in Nagasaki after the Russo-Japanese War (1904-5) and many enterprises run by foreigners either folded or moved to greener pastures, but Holme, Ringer & Co. remained and went on to enjoy a virtual monopoly on international business in western Japan.[140]

The Oura Bund, Opposite English Consul, Nagasaki.　り 通岸海浦大　崎長

Fig.6-2 A picture postcard published circa 1915 shows the Holme, Ringer & Co. office (right) and Nagasaki British Consulate at No. 7 and No. 6 Ōura. The Nagasaki American Consulate would move into the building on the far left in 1921. (Private collection)

---

[140] For further information see: Brian Burke-Gaffney, *Holme, Ringer & Company: The Rise and Fall of a British Enterprise in Japan, 1868-1940*. Brill, 2013.

Fig.6-3a,b (Above) The members of the Nagasaki Club pose for a photograph circa 1935. The tall man in the back row is Ferdinand C. Greatrex. Freddy and Sydney Ringer are seated at the far left and center, respectively. Sydney's sons Vanya and Michael are standing in the rear. (Below) Nagasaki officials and scholars gathered at the Nagasaki Library circa 1933 to welcome British historian Charles R. Boxer (light-colored suit), serving at the time as an exchange officer in the Imperial Japanese Army and visiting Nagasaki to conduct research for his book *Jan Compagnie in Japan* (1936). Ferdinand C. Greatrex is sitting with his legs crossed. The man seated at the far left is the renowned Nagasaki historian Koga Jūjirō.

As Nagasaki's foremost foreign resident and businessman, Frederick Ringer served as a merchant consul and represented several countries including Belgium, Norway, Sweden and the Hawaiian Republic. As mentioned earlier in the present work, he provoked the ire of the official British consul by claiming the right to seniority based on his longer stay in Nagasaki. After Ringer's death in England in 1907, his two sons Freddy and Sydney continued the family business and succeeded agencies and consular appointments. When the Shimonoseki British Consulate closed in 1922, the British manager of Wuriu Shokwai assumed the position of consular agent, and the company even moved into the former consulate building in Karato-chō. By the mid-1930s, Frederick Ringer's grandsons (Sydney's sons) Michael and Vanya were poised to join the company as junior partners.

In May 1935, Ferdinand C. Greatrex and the Ringer family led the British community of Nagasaki in celebrating the silver anniversary of the coronation of King George V of England. Greatrex adhered to the old custom in the port and threw open the consulate for congratulatory visits by Japanese officials and other guests. He also officiated at a Church of England service held at the Holy Trinity Church in Ōmura-machi. Freddy and Sydney Ringer meanwhile hosted a garden party and fancy dress ball in their hillside residences at No.14 and No.2 Minamiyamate, respectively. The organizers had to move the events forward to May 5, the day before the actual anniversary, because all the local clergymen were required to attend a general synod in Sendai. As a result, the Nagasaki celebration was hailed as the first in the British Empire. The author of a newspaper report on the garden party described the Ringer family house at No. 14 Minamiyamate as "not only a beautiful place, but one that was especially appropriate owing to the long connection of the family with the port and the many occasions when it has been similarly used by the British community."[141] The parties, attended by a large number of both Japanese and foreign residents, seemed to confirm the longstanding relationship of international trust and friendship in Nagasaki, but it was destined to be one of the last gestures of British-Japanese solidarity.

As the business fortunes of Nagasaki declined and relations between Britain and Japan showed increasing signs of strain, the British consulate and Holme, Ringer & Co. office stood side by side on the Nagasaki waterfront like a pair of bullfinches huddling together on a branch during a cold snap, one a center for social and diplomatic activity, the other the last pillar of international business in the port.

---

[141] *The Japan Chronicle*, May 10, 1935.

り 通 岸 海 浦 大 崎 長
Oura Pier Nagasaki. (昭和9.11.22長崎要塞司令部検閲済)

Fig.6-4 The Nagasaki Bund captured in a picture postcard circa 1934. The buildings (from left to right) are the American Consulate, British Consulate, Holme, Ringer & Co. office and the recently-opened Europa Hotel. The large building on the hillside is Kwassui Women's School at No. 13 Higashiyamate, the lot formerly reserved for the British Consulate. The title incorrectly identifies the waterfront as a pier. The Japanese inscription to the lower right reads "Passed by Nagasaki Fortress Headquarters censors on November 22, 1934," hinting at the heightened security in Nagasaki and the looming threat of confrontation between Japan and the countries of the West. (Private collection)

In the Shadow of War

Ferdinand C. Greatrex took a leave of absence in 1936 and gave the reins of the Nagasaki consulate to Henry H. Thomas, a graduate of Cambridge University and a new face in the Japan Consular Service. During his sojourn, Thomas revived the discussion about the value of maintaining the Nagasaki consulate when the port had long since been eclipsed commercially and politically by Fukuoka. He made a courtesy call to the Fukuoka Prefecture Office and tried to establish a link with government officials, but he wrote later to the British ambassador in Tokyo reporting the unfriendly attitude he had encountered there and his failed attempts to acquire information about public works and commercial enterprises. This, he said, was in "marked contrast to the Prefectural and Municipal authorities in Nagasaki, of the Customs authorities in both Nagasaki and Moji, and of the Shimonoseki Municipality, which I have found to be entirely friendly and even cordial." Thomas concluded his report with the following comment:

I do not necessarily grumble at the withholding of the information. It is just possible that the Municipality may be genuinely under the impression that they have a good and sufficient reason for withholding it. What is, however, so undesirable is the very marked lack of even the scantiest consideration and courtesy toward the British Consulate.[142]

During his stay in England in 1936, Ferdinand C. Greatrex signed papers in the High Court of Justice agreeing to a divorce from his wife Alys, whom he had left in England with their two sons the previous decade. In her "Petition for Dissolution of Marriage," Alys claimed that Greatrex had frequently committed adultery with "Miss Margaret Sharpe."[143] Little is known about the British consul's private life, but the *Japan Directory* shows Sharpe, a native of Kansas, working as a correspondence clerk in the Nagasaki American Consulate from the year 1931. In December 1937, Greatrex and Sharpe officially wed in a ceremony in the British Consulate. He was fifty-three and she was forty-two years old at the time.

Another largely undocumented activity of Ferdinand C. Greatrex was his research in the field of botany, apparently pursued in parallel to his long career in the Japan Consular Service. Greatrex made frequent trips to the countryside near Nagasaki to identify and record unusual plants, and one rare species of violet that he discovered at Unzen was even named in his honor: *Viola greatrexii* Nakai & Maek.[144]

The atmosphere of animosity and secrecy hampering international relations in Nagasaki only deepened after the outbreak of war between Japan and China in July 1937. The Japanese government initiated a movement to enhance national unity and ordered the establishment of civilian defense headquarters in city halls around the country to supervise blackout simulations and anti-air raid drills. It also enacted the New Military Secrets Protection Law, which gave authorities far-reaching powers to arrest and detain anyone suspected of collecting sensitive information or leaking military secrets.[145] The government tightened the screws further in March the following year by enacting the National Mobilization Law (*kokkasōdōin-hō*), a draconian edict that placed Japan firmly on an arc to war by limiting freedom of speech in the media, extending government control to all civilian organizations including labor unions, and making war production the highest priority in budget allocations.

---

[142] Henry H. Thomas to Sir John Tilley, September 15, 1936 (FO 262/2010).
[143] National Archives of the UK, J 77-3614-2022.
[144] http://plants.jstor.org/person/bm000003160
[145] The British Ambassador to Japan sent a circular to his consuls in Nagasaki and other ports providing an English translation of the new law and advising them to warn all British subjects about its purport. (FO 796/197)

The same month, a ceremony was held at the Mitsubishi Nagasaki Shipyard to mark the beginning of a project to build the mammoth 70,000-ton battleship *Musashi*.[146] Mitsubishi Company reinforced and modified the No. 2 building berth, added auxiliary facilities and equipment, and mobilized thousands of workers under a strict oath of secrecy. Authorities hid the building berth from view behind rope curtains and rolled out a tight blanket of security to ensure that outsiders, particularly foreigners, remained unaware of the activity in the shipyard. They also filled in a strip of land along the Ōura waterfront and constructed a row of warehouses—nick-named *mekakushi sōko* (blindfold warehouses)—to block the view of the shipyard from the row of buildings facing the harbor in the former foreign settlement, which included the American Consulate, British Consulate and Holme, Ringer & Co. office at Nos. 5, 6 and 7 Ōura, respectively. Anything left of the peaceful and cosmopolitan port of Nagasaki disappeared into the shadow of the city's new role as a military stronghold.

Fig.6-5 The former Nagasaki Bund is shown in a photograph taken by American Occupation forces in October 1945. The warehouses to the left were built to block the view of the Mitsubishi Nagasaki Shipyard from the American and British consulates. (US National Archives)

[146] Senkan musashi kenzō kiroku kankōiinkai, ed., *Senkan musashi kenzō kiroku: yamatogata senkan no zenbō* (The Construction of the 'Musashi': A Portrait of the Yamato-class Battleships) (Tokyo: Atene Shobo, 1994).

By 1940 the tension was reaching breaking point. Freddy Ringer died in Nagasaki in February at the age of fifty-six, his demise probably hastened by the deterioration of British-Japanese relations. In July, his nephews Michael and Vanya Ringer were arrested and jailed during a nationwide crackdown on an alleged spy ring, which in practical terms meant any British, Dutch or American businessman brazen enough to linger in Japan. Finally released from jail in September, the two left Japan to join the British Indian Army. Their father Sydney had managed to escape incarceration because of his consular credentials, but he closed the Holme, Ringer & Co. offices the following month and fled with his wife to Shanghai, where the couple were destined to spend the war in civilian concentration camps.

NAGASAKI

CONSULATES

American Consulate
(Nagasaki Office Closed)

Brazilian Consulate
c/o Chamber of Commerce Bldg., Sakura-machi
Tel.: 29 and 2024
Yutaka Ota, *Consul*

British Consulate
(Also in charge of Netherlands & Norwegian interests)
6 Oura
Tel.: 897. P.O. Box 16. Tel. Add.: "Britain." Nagasaki
F. C. Greatrex, *Consul*
S. Nakayama, *Shipping Clerk*

Danish Consulate
(See under American Consulate)

French Consular Agency
(Closed)

Norwegian Consulate, Royal
7 Oura
Tel.: 218
V. Ringer, *Consul*

Portuguese Consulate
7 Oura
Tel.: 218. P.O. Box 22
V. Ringer, *Acting Vice-Consul*

Swedish Consulate
(Closed)

Nagasaki Court of Appeal
Manzai-machi
Tel.: 438. 2294

Nagasaki Custom-house
Hagoromo-cho 2-chome
Tel.: 4400-02

Nagasaki District Court
Manzai-machi
Tel.: 0240

Nagasaki Forestry Office
Higashi Kami-machi
Tel.: 1196

Nagasaki Local Court
Manzai-machi

Nagasaki Municipal Office
36 Sakura-machi
Tel.: 0002, 0880, 0988, 3700-06

Nagasaki Police Station
Yedo-machi
Tel.: 7, 989

Nagasaki Post Office
Megasaki
Tel.: 6

Nagasaki Prefectural Library
Kaminishiyama-cho
Tel.: 3684

Nagasaki Prefectural Office
Sotoura-machi
Tel.: 3300-11, 3807, 3814
Kawanishi Jitsuzo, *Governor*

Nagasaki Tax Office
Motodaiku-machi

Fig.6-6 The 1940 issue of the *Japan Directory* (published annually in Hong Kong) shows only Ferdinand C. Greatrex and Sydney Ringer's son Vanya remaining in Nagasaki as foreign consular representatives.

Ferdinand and Margaret Greatrex remained in the British Consulate at No. 6 Ōura, reading newspaper reports about the Luftwaffe air raids on London and the Tripartite Pact signed by Germany, Italy and Japan in September 1940. American Consul Arthur F. Tower left Nagasaki at the end of June 1941 for Kobe, but Ferdinand C. Greatrex stuck to his desk in the British Consulate like a captain refusing to abandon the helm of a sinking ship. When news of the Pearl Harbor attack and Japan's declaration of war reached Nagasaki on December 8, 1941, military police surrounded the consulate, placed Greatrex and his wife under house arrest, and forced Konishi Kizō to quit the premises. The same day, Freddy Ringer's widow Alcidie was arrested at her home in Minamiyamate and marched off to the Umegasaki Police Station for interrogation.

Ferdinand and Margaret Greatrex and Alcidie Ringer were later confined in a school on the outskirts of Nagasaki along with a few intrepid missionaries, elderly men with Japanese wives, and other enemy nationals who had ignored the injunctions to leave Japan. In July 1942, the three were finally allowed to leave the city and to travel to Yokohama to board an exchange ship with other stranded Britons undergoing repatriation. Before leaving Nagasaki, Greatrex appointed Ikegami Heizō, a veteran employee of Holme, Ringer & Co., to serve as caretaker of the Nagasaki British Consulate, and the latter took up residence with his family in the former shipping clerk's quarters at the rear of the property. The consul also asked that his personal belongings—including a car, piano, furniture and electrical appliances—be delivered to his faithful servant Konishi Kizō, who had moved to Shiga Prefecture.

For the rest of World War Two, the Nagasaki British Consulate and other Allied government property in Japan remained under the wing of the neutral Swiss Legation in Tokyo. The protection did not extend, however, to personal belongings. The Japanese government passed a law in March 1942 to convert all the perpetual leases still in effect in the former foreign settlements into ownership rights. The authorities then sold off most of the land and buildings owned by enemy nationals (without their knowledge or consent) and deposited the funds in bank accounts administered by government-appointed custodians. The rights to almost all of the twenty lots owned by the Ringer family, including the Holme, Ringer & Co. office at No. 7 Ōura and the houses in Minamiyamate, were transferred by the summer of 1943 and the buildings occupied by new Japanese owners.

Despite the animosity and xenophobia gripping Japan, none of the buildings on the Ōura waterfront—including the British consulate, Holme, Ringer & Co. office and American consulate—suffered any harm at the hands of patriots or vandals. In fact, the greatest wartime damage was inflicted by the atomic bomb, which plunged from the belly of an American B29 bomber one hot summer morning in August 1945 and exploded four kilometers to the north, generating a ferocious blast that smashed windows and ripped off parts of the old rooftops in the former Nagasaki Foreign Settlement.

7 POSTWAR EPILOGUE

THE ATOMIC BOMBING of August 9, 1945 reduced the northern half of Nagasaki to rubble and killed or injured more than two-thirds of the city population. The neighborhoods north of Nagasaki Railway Station bore the brunt of destruction, but much of the urban core also succumbed to secondary fires rampaging through the city in the aftermath. The former foreign settlement lay at a relatively safe distance from the hypocenter and enjoyed the protection of hills and canals, but many of the old Western-style buildings had already been demolished during the war to create firebreaks, and the ones still standing, including the former British Consulate building at No. 6 Ōura, looked like the broken relics of a forgotten era.

After their arrival in Nagasaki in September 1945, the Allied Occupation forces conducted an investigation regarding Allied property seized by Japanese authorities, including the personal belongings of former British Consul Ferdinand C. Greatrex and his wife either left at the consulate or given to their servant Konishi Kizō. The list drawn up with the assistance of Japanese authorities shows that Konishi had taken possession of the consul's car, a Chrysler saloon, in May 1943 but that he had been ordered to give it to the Yanase automobile importing company. By October 1946, the car had found its way to Ibaragi Prefecture and was still being used by the prefecture office. Most of Greatrex's furniture and appliances had been sold arbitrarily to Nonaka Chūta, a former coal baron who had established a school for women in Takeo, Saga Prefecture.[147] Greatrex's last communication with the Allied authorities in Japan was a request that the proceeds from the sale of property and the rest of the money in his account at the Yokohama Specie Bank be transferred to Konishi Kizō.

---

[147] Record Group 331, UD1610, File No.3840, U.S. National Archives (NARA), College Park.

Ferdinand C. Greatrex retired from the consular service in 1943 and later moved to Southern Rhodesia (Zimbabwe), where he continued his work as a botanist. His wife Margaret became an activist for women's rights in Africa, serving as president of the Federation of Women's Institutes of Southern Rhodesia.

British authorities conducted their first inspection of the former Nagasaki British Consulate in late February 1946. A member of the UK Liaison Mission (the British representation in Japan prior to the revival of the embassy) named G.H.D. Bell traveled by train from Tokyo to Nagasaki and visited the premises, where he met Ikegami Heizō and checked the contents of the buildings using lists compiled in 1944 by the Swiss Legation. Bell later submitted a report on the state of the various rooms and the contents of unlocked cupboards, bookshelves and closets. He found that the consulate telephone was missing, that a few seals had been broken, and that the stationery closet had been ransacked, but otherwise he concluded that most of the consular archives and moveable property identified previously by the Swiss inspectors were intact. He was appalled nevertheless by the miserable overall condition of the buildings:

> In short the shell of the building is in good condition, but the tiled roofs, inside decorations and builders' fittings are in a very bad condition. All this is definitely the result of bomb blast. Much time, labour and material would be required to put the building in order and fit for official work, and as a residence for government officials. The servants' quarters in the compound also are damaged considerably, and definitely uninhabitable. The house in which the custodian lives with his family is in a deplorable condition, despite the various attempts to make the house tenantable by replacing doors, glass to windows, etc. at his own expense.[148]

On March 16 the same year, Clement H. Archer of the UK Liaison Mission and Paul Wurth, representative of the Swiss Legation, signed an official "Protocol of Transfer of the Archives and Furniture of H.B.M. Consulate in Nagasaki" and submitted a copy to the Foreign Office in London along with an eighteen-page inventory.[149] In an accompanying

---

[148] Report on an inspection of the British consular premises in Nagasaki and Shimonoseki by G.H.D. Bell, March 6, 1946 (FO 366/1541)

[149] FO 366/1541. The inventory ends with an addendum listing a number of records—including the archive files for the years 1938 to 1941 and F.C. Greatrex's diaries—purportedly seized by Japanese authorities in December 1941 but delivered by them to the Swiss Legation in August 1942 and later deposited in the British Embassy. However, these records cannot be found today.

Fig.7-1,a,b (Above) The Allied Occupation forces took photographs of the former Nagasaki American Consulate soon after the war's end. The "blindfold warehouses" are still standing directly in front of the American and British (left) consulates. (Below) The former Holme, Ringer & Co. office, adjacent to the British Consulate, was destroyed by fire in April 1947 while in use by Occupation forces. The property was later purchased by the Nagasaki Bus Company and converted into a parking lot. (US National Archives)

letter, Archer reported that he had arranged to have the consulate buildings boarded up and that he had engaged Ikegami Heizō to remain on the premises as caretaker.

Fig.7-2 Sydney Ringer relaxes with Ikegami Heizō (far right) and his family circa 1952. Ringer returned to Japan after internment in Shanghai and sold off the family properties in Nagasaki and Shimonoseki. He died in England in 1967. (Courtesy of Elizabeth Newton)

Disposal of the Consulate Buildings

The British government disbanded the Japan Consular Service at the height of World War Two, bringing an end to a system of diplomatic representation dating back to the opening of Japan's doors in 1859. Ferdinand C. Greatrex and many of his colleagues retired at this point; others remained in the employ of the Foreign Office and returned to Japan to assist in restoring bilateral relations. After the San Francisco Peace Treaty—signed on September 8, 1951 and effectuated in April the following year—Japan began a new era of economic recovery in cooperation with the countries of the West. British authorities re-established the embassy in Tokyo and opened consulates in Yokohama and Osaka with the assistance of the Japanese government.

It was clear from the outset that, however steeped in history and nostalgic significance, the former Nagasaki British Consulate was no longer needed. In March 1952, Sir Esler Dening—soon to be appointed the first postwar British ambassador to Japan—wrote from Tokyo to the Foreign Office in London reporting on a visit to Nagasaki and expressing his opinion that: "The importance of Nagasaki has been declining steadily in recent years and I see no prospect of a revival which would justify the re-opening of a British consular post. I therefore recommend that since Her Majesty's Government are unlikely to have any further use for the premises, and since it would cost a considerable sum to put them into rentable condition, arrangements should be made for them to be sold."[150]

Dening's opinion, as well as information that shipping had increased in the Shimonoseki/Moji area and that Holme, Ringer & Co. had reopened in Moji, prompted a decision by the Foreign Office to abandon the former Nagasaki consulate and to appoint Thomas Malcolm, the area manager of Holme, Ringer & Co., to serve as British consular agent with responsibility for all of western Japan. Subsequently, signs saying British Consular Agency and British Consular Residence appeared on the doorways of the Holme, Ringer & Co. office in Moji and Malcolm's house on the Shimonoseki hillside.[151]

The first issue that British and Japanese representatives had to address was implementation of the various clauses in the San Francisco Peace Treaty. One of the most vexing was Article 15, which enjoined Japan to return all Allied property seized during the war and to provide compensation for wartime damage according to the Allied Powers Property Compensation Law approved earlier by the Japanese Cabinet. Soon after the ratification of the treaty, the British Foreign Office launched negotiations with the Japanese Ministry of Foreign Affairs regarding the various government properties in Japan, including the former consular premises in Nagasaki.

In June 1953, Japan agreed to pay 5,780,654 yen as compensation for damages suffered by the Nagasaki British Consulate. The sum was equivalent to about half of the market value of the property, rather exorbitant in view of the fact that an American bomb had caused most of the damage in question and that Japanese authorities had already conducted some repair work. Moreover, the money apparently went right into the coffers of the British Treasury, not into any sort of project to restore the consulate to its

---

[150] Sir Esler Dening to the Foreign Office, March 21, 1952 (FO 262/2082)

[151] The Ringer family participated only nominally in the postwar revival of Holme, Ringer & Co. Thomas Malcolm and his successors lived in Sydney A. Ringer's former Shimonoseki residence, which is in use today as the Fujiwara Yoshie Memorial Museum. The former consulate building was sold to Shimonoseki City in 1954 and remains as a National Important Cultural Property.

former beauty.[152]

A representative of the Commissioner of Works visited Nagasaki the same month to make arrangements for the sale of the property. He called at the local branch of the Nippon Kangyō Bank and inquired about the market value of the land and buildings at No. 6 Ōura. The estimate presented by the bank was 11.7 million yen, based on current land assessments. The British Embassy in Tokyo relayed this information to the Foreign Office along with the following report:

> On June 29, the Mayor of Nagasaki called at the Chancery to express surprise and dismay at the news that we were proposing to sell the consular property at Nagasaki; he claimed to have learnt this only recently. The mayor expressed interest in purchasing the building from us and holding it against the day when we might wish to re-open the consulate in Nagasaki. He wanted to know the price we were asking. We wrote to the mayor on July 8 confirming that our decision to sell was irrevocable and permanent and implying that we would not consider the mayor's offer to hold the consular building against a possible re-opening. We informed the mayor of the valuation of Yen 11,700,000 mentioned above, and asked him what price he might be prepared to offer. We also told the mayor that interest in the property had already been shown by a Father Thomas P. Purcell, an American Roman Catholic priest of the Order of St. Augustine, who wishes to acquire the British consular building as a boys' school. Father Purcell has so far only offered us U.S.$10,000. Although there would be political advantage in helping the Augustinians to settle in that part of Japan, we doubt whether such a figure would be acceptable even if we do not at once receive a better offer.[153]

In a subsequent letter, the embassy reported that the mayor had visited the embassy again to ask for a reduction in the price, pointing out that the building "is in a bad state of disrepair, and it will cost many thousands of yen to repair." The chancery official writing the letter seemed to agree with the mayor's argument:

> Colour is lent to this assertion by the fact that we are receiving Yen 5,780,654 under the Allied Powers Property Compensation Law. The mayor went on to say that the municipality has decided to repair and maintain the building as an important historical relic, perhaps to be used as

---

[152] Tsuruga Shichizo (International Cooperation Bureau, Japanese Ministry of Foreign Affairs) to Cooper Blyth (Commercial Secretariat, British Embassy, Tokyo), June 4, 1953 (WORK 10/359).

[153] Chancery, British Embassy, Tokyo to the Conference and Supply Department, Foreign Office, London, August 10, 1953 (WORK 10/359).

a children's reading room. Would we not, in view of all this, make some contribution towards the cost, or, at any rate, accept a lower figure? We explained that we had no discretion to come to any binding agreement without your authority, but suggested that it might perhaps go some way toward meeting the municipality's difficulties if we sought permission to sell for Yen 10,000,000. This seemed to be wholly acceptable to the mayor and we hope that you too will see no objection. Perhaps you could send us a brief telegram in order that we may let him know.[154]

The British Embassy in Tokyo supported the opinion that the sale at a reduced price to Nagasaki City would strengthen British-Japanese friendship and facilitate efforts to promote British interests in the region. The Foreign Office concurred, adding in a letter to the Ministry of Works that, "this transaction should not be treated as a purely commercial matter as our relations with Japan are not so cordial that we can afford to pass up opportunities of fostering pro-British feeling."[155] However, the Treasury, which had the final say in the matter, placed the monetary value of the property above diplomatic considerations. An official of the Ministry of Works wrote to the Foreign Office on May 22, 1954 relaying the following instructions:

[The final] decision is that there is not sufficient justification for departing from the normal rule that we should get as much as we can from the property. Will you please therefore instruct the Embassy at Tokyo to put the property up for sale and to report the results to us? I was glad to have your assurances in your letter of 23rd April that the Post had in no way committed themselves to the mayor of Nagasaki.[156]

The British Embassy responded by advertising the sale of the former Nagasaki British Consulate in Nagasaki and Osaka. The Nagasaki Bus Company, which had purchased the former Holme, Ringer & Co. office lot next door for use as parking space, nibbled on the line at one point but eventually withdrew. No other serious buyer came forward. Finally on October 12, the British Embassy issued two letters, one a note to the Foreign Office expressing the opinion that "we are fortunate that the municipality are interested in the property as a 'historic monument,' otherwise I doubt whether we should have got near the figure we are now offered," and the other a message to Tagawa Tsutomu, mayor of Nagasaki, accepting the latter's offer of 10 million yen for the consulate property.

The decision to accept the mayor's offer caused a stir in the hallways of

---

[154] Ibid, November 24, 1953.
[155] F.J. Gaunt to M.G. Bradley, March 3, 1954 (WORK 10/359).
[156] R.B. Marshall to J. McAdam Clark, May 22, 1954 (WORK 10/359).

the Foreign Office and Ministry of Works because it had not been finalized in the upper echelons of government, but in the end the transaction was approved as a *fait accompli*. Embassy officials handed over the keys to the property in June 1955, and in November the embassy's administration section reported to the Foreign Office that the money had been duly received from Nagasaki City and posted in current accounts. The final document in the Ministry of Works folder regarding the Nagasaki British Consulate is a blank page with a red stamp bearing the words: "Closed, no further action to be taken."

The Former Nagasaki British Consulate Today

After the change of guard, Nagasaki city authorities conducted the much-awaited repairs to the former consulate. Part of the main building was earmarked for use as an office of the municipal education department, while the former drawing room and dining room as well as the living space upstairs were decorated with posters, showcases and exhibits in preparation for the opening of the Nagasaki Children's Science Museum in April 1957.

The new facility and the old brick building accommodating it stimulated the imagination of generations of school children, but little effort was made to highlight the history of the Nagasaki British Consulate or the stories of the people who once lived and worked there. By the time the museum closed in 1990, few people in Nagasaki could remember the consulate in its heyday, let alone decipher the insignia *EVIIR* inscribed on the fireplace mantels in tribute to King Edward VII, during whose reign the building had been erected.

Museum paraphernalia were still being removed from the premises when the Japanese national government designated the former Nagasaki British Consulate an Important Cultural Property, guaranteeing its preservation as a heritage site. The principal reason for the designation was that the former consulate—including the main building, outbuildings and gardens—had not been significantly altered since the time of construction and therefore presented a valuable example of Western-style architecture of the late Meiji Period.

The following year, the Japanese government marked off an urban zone called the Higashiyamate and Minamiyamate Historic Preservation District and ensured that the unique architectural heritage of the former Nagasaki Foreign Settlement—albeit reduced from some 800 buildings at its peak to less than 50 in 1991—would be preserved and passed along to future generations.

Fig.7-4a,b The former Nagasaki British Consulate, front and rear views.

Tomorrow and Beyond

The only building in the Ōura neighborhood included in the historic preservation district was the former Nagasaki British Consulate. As a result, office buildings, condominiums and hotels of modern construction appeared nearby, severing any connection the former consulate may have shared with the surrounding neighborhoods, like the little house in the Virginia Lee Burton story of the same title that sinks wearily into the shadow of urban sprawl.

The warehouses thrown up to block the view of the harbor on the eve of World War Two eventually disappeared, but the land reclamations conducted later to create space for Mizubenomori Park virtually erased any lingering image of the former consulate facing directly onto the water.

After closing the Nagasaki Children's Science Museum, the Nagasaki Municipal Council puzzled over the best way to use the building, especially now that the designation of Important Cultural Property had saved it from the brink of destruction but imposed a number of restrictions on any modification that might jeopardize its architectural integrity. In 1993, the city elders passed a motion to open an art gallery exhibiting the work of the late Noguchi Yatarō, who hailed from Nagasaki Prefecture and left a number of paintings depicting Nagasaki Harbor and scenes from the former foreign settlement. The new facility gained a niche in the local tourism industry but did little more than its predecessor to shed light on the former Nagasaki British Consulate.

In 2007, the municipal government decided to move the art gallery to a different location in the city and to conduct still another facelift, this time not only cosmetic repairs but also groundwork to resolve the buildings' inherent susceptibility to earthquakes. It is hoped that this time around the building will be used, not only as an architectural specimen, but also as a vehicle for information about the role of the consulate in the boom years of the late nineteenth and early twentieth centuries, the life and work of former consuls, and the contributions made by British residents to the industrial, economic and cultural development of Nagasaki.

Appendix I
BRITISH CONSULS IN NAGASAKI (1859-1941)

1859	C. Pemberton Hodgson (acting)
1859-1863	George S. Morrison
1861	Francis G. Myburgh (acting)
1862	Charles A. Winchester (acting)
1864	Francis G. Myburgh
1864-1866	Abel A.J. Gower
1866-1877	Marcus O. Flowers
1877-1882	James Troup
1882-1883	John C. Hall (acting)
1883-1884	William G. Aston
1884	John C. Hall (acting)
1884	Frank W. Playfair (acting)
1884	W.A. Woolley (acting)
1884-1889	James J. Enslie
1889-1896	John J. Quin
1890-1892	John C. Hall (acting)
1896-1897	Ralph G.E. Forster (acting)
1897-1901	Joseph H. Longford
1901-1902	Ralph G.E. Forster (acting)
1902-1905	E. Hamilton Holmes (acting)
1905-1909	Frank W. Playfair
1905-1906	Harold G. Parlett (acting)
1909-1912	Arthur M. Chalmers
1912-1913	Ralph G. Forster
1914-1915	John B. Rentiers
1915-1918	John T. Wawn
1918-1920	Thomas J. Harrington
1918-1919	Robert Boulter (acting)
1920-1924	Oswald White
1923	Reginald McPherson Austin
1924-1927	Montague B.T. Paske-Smith
1927-1941	Ferdinand C. Greatrex
1936	Henry H. Thomas (acting)

Appendix II
NAGASAKI BRITISH CONSULATE CHRONOLOGY

1859	June 13. C. Pemberton Hodgson opens the Nagasaki British Consulate at Myōgyōji Temple and hoists the Union Jack for the first time in Japan.
	August. George S. Morrison arrives in Nagasaki and takes over for Hodgson, who proceeds to Hakodate.
1861	June 22. *The Nagasaki Shipping List and Advertiser* is designated the Official Organ of all Notifications proceeding from Her Britannic Majesty's Legation, Consulate General, and Consulates in Japan (the newspaper moves to Yokohama in October the same year).
	September. George S. Morrison returns to England on leave of absence, and Francis G. Myburgh takes over as acting consul.
1862	July. Charles A. Winchester takes over for F.G. Myburgh as acting consul.
1863	April. George S. Morrison returns to Nagasaki.
	June. George S. Morrison moves the consulate to Green's Hotel at No. 11 Minamiyamate (directly below Myōgyōji), renting the building for two years at $1,800 per annum.
	September. George S. Morrison retires from the Japan Consular Service, and Francis G. Myburgh takes over as acting consul at Nagasaki.
1864	February. Francis G. Myburgh is officially appointed consul at Nagasaki.
	May. Abel A.J. Gower takes over as consul and Francis G. Myburgh proceeds to Kobe.

1865	July. Abel A.J. Gower moves the consulate to No. 9 Higashiyamate, renting the two-story building from Glover & Co. (representatives for Dent & Co., holders of the perpetual lease) for $150 per month.
1866	February. Marcus O. Flowers takes over as consul and Abel A.J. Gower proceeds to Hakodate.
1867	August. Two British sailors on the HMS *Icarus* are murdered in Nagasaki, and Marcus O. Flowers heads the subsequent investigation. The incident contributes to the Meiji Restoration the following year.
1870	Marcus O. Flowers presides over the liquidation of Glover & Co. in the consular court.
1877	November. James Troup takes over as consul at Nagasaki, and Marcus O. Flowers proceeds to Kobe.
1882	March. The British consulate moves from No. 9 Higashiyamate to No.6 Ōura. The stone warehouse at the rear of the property is converted into a consular jail. James Troup is appointed consul at Kobe, and John C. Hall takes over as acting consul at Nagasaki.
1883	December. William G. Aston is appointed consul at Nagasaki. John C. Hall remains in Nagasaki as assistant.
1884	April. William G. Aston is appointed acting British consul-general in Korea, and John C. Hall takes over as acting consul at Nagasaki.
	September. John C. Hall is appointed assistant Japanese secretary to the British Legation at Tokyo. Frank W. Playfair and W.A. Woolley take over as acting consul at Nagasaki in September and November, respectively.
	September 2. Charles Sutton sells the buildings at No. 6 Ōura for $2,130 and transfers the perpetual lease to Her British Majesty's First Commissioner of Works.

	December 31. James J. Enslie takes over as British consul at Nagasaki.
1885	December 19. A notice is posted in *The Rising Sun and Nagasaki Express* announcing the sale of the former British consulate properties at Nos.8, 9 and 10 Higashiyamate. At the public auction held in January 1886, the Reformed Church in America purchases Lots No. 9 and No. 10 for $510 and $150, respectively. The church also acquires lot No. 8 later the same year.
1889	February. John J. Quin takes over as British consul at Nagasaki, and James J. Enslie proceeds to Kobe.
1890	November. John J. Quin takes a long leave of absence. John C. Hall returns to take up the position of British consul at Nagasaki.
1892	February. John J. Quin resumes the post of British consul at Nagasaki.
1896	June. John J. Quin takes a leave of absence. Ralph G.E. Forster is appointed acting consul. Quin dies in Ireland the following year.
1897	January. Joseph H. Longford is appointed British consul at Nagasaki and moves into the Glover family residence at No. 3 Minamiyamate with his wife and four children.
1901	April. Joseph H. Longford takes a leave of absence and Ralph G.E. Forster takes over as acting consul. Longford retires from the Japan Consular Service the following year to accept an appointment as the first professor of Japanese at King's College London.
1902	October. Ralph G.E. Forster is transferred to the Hakodate consulate and E. Hamilton Holmes takes over as acting consul. William Cowan, British Surveyor of Works in Shanghai, recommends the rebuilding of the Nagasaki consular premises.
1904	October 8. E. Hamilton Holmes moves the consulate to a temporary building at No. 47 Sagarimatsu, formerly the office of

	the Chinese Eastern Railway Company owned by the China and Japan Trading Company. The rent is 75 yen/month. The dilapidated buildings at No. 6 Ōura are later demolished in preparation for the construction of a new consulate.
1905	January. Frank W. Playfair is appointed British consul at Nagasaki. E. Hamilton Holmes proceeds to Seoul.
	May. William Cowan submits architectural plans to the Foreign Office for new consulate buildings at Nagasaki. The buildings originally planned are reduced in scale as a cost-saving measure.
1906	August. Nagasaki contractor Gotō Kametarō is engaged to construct the new consulate. The contract calls for a payment of 50,000 yen in installments linked to the progress of the work.
1907	June. Gotō, suffering from financial difficulties, transfers the contract to Moritaka Ichidayū. Moritaka later threatens to set fire to the building unless his demands for more money are met. In the summer of the following year he accepts a severance payment of 3,000 yen, and the rest of the work is finished by day laborers. The total cost is £7,270, 27% more than the original estimate.
1908	November. Frank W. Playfair moves the British consulate into the new buildings.
1909	October. Frank W. Playfair retires from the Japan Consular Service. His successors at Nagasaki are Arthur M. Chalmers (1909-1912), Ralph G. Forster (1912-1913) and John B. Rentiers (1914-1915).
1915	January. John T. Wawn succeeds John B. Rentiers, who proceeds to Manila.
1918	April. Thomas J. Harrington is appointed to succeed John T. Wawn, but Robert Boulter serves as acting consul until his arrival here in February 1919. Wawn retires from the Japan Consular Service and settles in the Nagasaki area.

1920	January. Oswald White succeeds Thomas J. Harrington, who proceeds to Manila.
1924	October. Montague B.T. Paske-Smith succeeds Oswald White, who proceeds to Dairen, China.
1926	November. Frederick E.E. (Freddy) Ringer is appointed honorary vice-consul (grade II).
1927	December. Ferdinand C. Greatrex succeeds Montague B.T. Paske-Smith, who proceeds to Osaka.
1930	June. Sydney A. Ringer is appointed honorary vice-consul (grade II).
1931	October. The Foreign Office airs a proposal to close the Nagasaki consulate but eventually decides against it.
1940	February. Freddy Ringer dies in Nagasaki.
	October. Sydney A. Ringer and his family leave Nagasaki under duress.
1941	December. Ferdinand C. Greatrex and his wife Margaret are placed under house arrest on December 8, the day of the Pearl Harbor attack. They are confined in Nagasaki until July the following year. Ikegami Heizō is appointed caretaker of the consulate and takes up residence there. The Swiss Legation in Tokyo takes over administration of the property.
1945	August. The explosion of the atomic bomb damages the consulate buildings.
1946	February. British authorities conduct a formal inspection of the consulate.
	March. The UK Liaison Mission and Swiss Legation sign the Protocol of Transfer of the Archives and Furniture of H.B.M.

	Consulate in Nagasaki.
1952	March. Sir Esler Dening recommends the sale of the former Nagasaki consulate buildings.
1953	June. Japan pays Britain 5,780,654 yen as compensation for damages to the Nagasaki Consulate according to the Allied Powers Property Compensation Law. The Nippon Kangyō Bank estimates the value of the former Nagasaki Consulate property as 11.7 million yen. The Office of Works, Foreign Office and British Embassy begin procedures to sell the property.
1954	October. British authorities accept an offer of 10 million yen from Nagasaki City for the consulate property.
1955	June. Nagasaki City takes possession of the former Nagasaki British Consulate.
1957	April. Nagasaki City opens the Nagasaki Children's Science Museum in the former consulate buildings.
1990	March. The Nagasaki Children's Science Museum closes. The Japanese government designates the former Nagasaki British Consulate an Important Cultural Property.
1991	The former consulate property is included in the Higashiyamate and Minamiyamate Historic Preservation District established by the Japanese government.
1993	April. The Noguchi Yatarō Memorial Art Gallery opens in the main building of the former Nagasaki consulate.
2007	The Noguchi Yatarō Memorial Art Gallery closes. A large-scale project begins to restore and earthquake-proof the buildings of the former Nagasaki British Consulate.

BIBLIOGRAPHY

Alcock, Sir Rutherford. *The Capital of the Tycoon: A Narrative of a Three Years' Residence in Japan.* London: Longman, Green, Longman, Roberts, and Green, 1863.

Auslin, Michael R. *Negotiating with Imperialism: The Unequal Treaties and the Culture of Japanese Diplomacy.* Cambridge: Harvard University Press, 2004.

Barr, Pat. *The Deer Cry Pavilion: A Story of Westerners in Japan, 1868-1905.* London: Macmillan, 1968.

----------. *The Coming of the Barbarians: A Story of Western Settlement in Japan, 1853-1870.* London: Macmillan, 1967.

Beasley, William G. *Great Britain and the Opening of Japan 1834-1858.* London: The Japan Library, 1995.

----------. *Select Documents on Japanese Foreign Policy 1853-1868.* London: Oxford University Press, 1955.

Burke-Gaffney, Brian. *Nagasaki: The British Experience, 1854-1945.* Folkestone: Global Oriental, 2009.

----------. *Holme, Ringer & Company: The Rise and Fall of a British Enterprise in Japan, 1868-1940.* Brill, 2013.

Chang, Richard T. *The Justice of the Western Consular Courts in Nineteenth-Century Japan.* Westport: Greenwood Press, 1984.

Cobbing, Andrew. *Kyushu, Gateway to Japan: A Concise History.* Folkestone: Global Oriental, 2008.

Cortazzi, Hugh. *Victorians in Japan in and around the Treaty Ports.* London and Atlantic Highlands, NJ: The Athlone Press, 1988.

----------. *Britain and the 'Re-opening' of Japan: The Treaty of Yedo of 1858 and the Elgin Mission.* London: Japan Society Publications, 2008.

----------. "Royal Visits to Japan in the Meiji Period, 1868-1912" in *Britain and Japan: Biographical Portraits Vol.*II, Ian Nish ed. Routledge, 1997.

Cortazzi, Hugh and Gordon Daniels, eds. *Britain and Japan, 1859-1991: Themes and Personalities.* London and New York: Routledge, 1991.

Cortazzi, Hugh, Ian Nish, Peter Lowe, James E. Hoare, eds. *British Envoys in Japan, 1859-1972*. Folkestone: Global Oriental, 2004.

Earns, Lane. *Nagasaki kyoryūchi no seiyōjin* (Westerners in the Nagasaki Foreign Settlement). Nagasaki: Nagasaki Bunkensha, 2002.

----------. "The Foreign Settlement in Nagasaki, 1859-1869." *The Historian* Vol.56, No.3. Spring 1994.

Fox, Grace. *Britain and Japan, 1858-1883*. Oxford: Oxford University Press, 1969.

Hishitani Takehira, *Nagasaki kyoryūchi no kenkyū* (Research on the Nagasaki Foreign Settlement). Fukuoka: Kyushu University Press, 1988.

Hoare, J.E. "Britain's Japan Consular Service, 1859-1941," *Britain & Japan: Biographical Portraits Vol. II*. Ian Nish ed. The Japan Library, 1997.

----------. *Embassies in the East*. London and New York: Routledge, 1999.

Hodgson, C. Pemberton. *A Residence at Nagasaki and Hakodate in 1859-1860*. London: Richard Bentley, 1861.

Kataoka Yakichi. *Nihon Kirishitan Junkyōshi* (A History of Christian Persecutions in Japan). Jiji Tsushinsha, 1979.

Kobayashi, Masaru. *Nagasaki meiji yōkan* (Western-style Buildings of the Meiji Period in Nagasaki). Private publication, 1993.

Kuwata Masaru, *Kindai ni okeru chūnichi eikokugaikōkan* (British Diplomats in Japan, 1859-1945). Kobe: Mirume Shobo, 2003.

Lamb, W. Kaye. *Empress to the Orient*. Vancouver Maritime Museum Society, 1991.

Lowe, Peter. *Britain in the Far East: A Survey from 1819 to the Present*. London and New York: Longman Group, 1981.

McKay, Alexander. *Scottish Samurai: Thomas Blake Glover 1838-1911*. Edinburgh: Canongate Press, 1997.

Nagasaki City, ed. *Nagasaki shisei rokujūgonenshi* (A Sixty-Five-Year History of the Nagasaki Municipal Administration). Nagasaki, 1959.

----------. *Nagasaki shishi nenpyō* (Nagasaki City Chronology). Nagasaki, 1981.

----------. *Nagasaki genbaku sensaishi* (Record of the War Damages Caused by the Nagasaki Atomic Bombing). Tokyo: Iwanami Shoten, 1991.

Nagasaki City Board of Education, ed. *Nagasaki kyoryūchi: dentōteki kenzōbutsugun hozontaisaku chōsahōkokusho* (Nagasaki Foreign Settlement: Report on Measures for the Preservation of a Group of Traditional Buildings). Nagasaki, 1989.

----------. *Nagasaki koshashinshū kyoryūchihen* (Old Photographs of the Nagasaki Foreign Settlement). Nagasaki, 1995.

----------. *Higashiyamate, Minamiyamate no rekishitekiisan wo machizukuri ni ikasu tame ni* (Exploiting the Historic Assets of Higashiyamate and Minamiyamate in City-making). Nagasaki, 2004.

Nagasaki Prefecture, ed., *Nagasaki kyoryūchi gaikokujin meibo* (List of Foreign Residents of the Nagasaki Foreign Settlement). Nagasaki: Nagasaki Prefectural Library, 2004.

Nippon Yusen Kaisha (N.Y.K.) ed. *Nippon yūsen kaisha nanajūnenshi* (Seventy-Year History of the Nippon Yusen Kaisha). Tokyo, 1956.

Nish, Ian, ed. *Britain & Japan: Biographical Portraits.* Folkestone, Kent: The Japan Library, 1994-1999.

Nishi-Nippon Heavy Industries Co. Ltd. Nagasaki Shipyard ed. *Mitsubishi Nagasaki zōsenjoshi zokuhen* (History of the Mitsubishi Nagasaki Shipyard. Nagasaki, 1951.

Paske-Smith, M. *Western Barbarians in Japan and Formosa in Tokugawa Days, 1603-1868.* Kobe: J.L. Thompson and Co., 1927.

Prendergast, Hew D.V., Jaeschke, Helena and Rumball, Naomi. *A Lacquer Legacy at Kew: The Japanese Collection of John J. Quin.* University of Chicago Press, 2001.

Ruxton, Ian ed. *The Semi-Official Letters of British Envoy Sir Ernest Satow from Japan and China (1895-1906).* Japan: Lulu.com, 2007.

Sakamoto Katsuhiko. *Meiji no ijinkan* (Foreign Houses of the Meiji Period). Tokyo: Asahi Shimbunsha, 1965.

Satow, Ernest. *A Diplomat in Japan.* London: Seeley, Service & Co., 1921.

Shigefuji Takeo. *Nagasaki kyoryūchi to gaikokushōnin* (Nagasaki Foreign Settlement and Foreign Merchants). Tokyo: Kazama Shobo, 1967.

Smith, George, *Ten Weeks in Japan*. London, 1861.

Sugiyama Shinya, *Meiji ishin to igirisu shōnin: tomasu gurabā no shōgai* (The Meiji Restoration and a British Merchant: The Life of Thomas B. Glover). Tokyo: Iwanami Shoten, 1993.

Taniguchi Ryōhei. *Mrs. Mary Elizabeth Green*. Unpublished Japanese manuscript, May 2010.

Wood, Frances. *No Dogs & Not Many Chinese: Treaty Port Life in China 1843-1943*. London: John Murray Ltd., 1998.

Yamaguchi Mitsuomi. *Nagasaki no yōfū kenchiku* (Western-style Architecture in Nagasaki). Nagasaki: Nagasaki City Board of Education, 1967.

ABOUT THE AUTHOR

Brian Burke-Gaffney was born in Winnipeg, Canada in 1950 and came to Japan in 1972, going on to train for nine years as an ordained monk of the Rinzai Zen Sect. He left the monastery and moved to Nagasaki in 1982. He is currently professor of cultural history at the Nagasaki Institute of Applied Science and honorary director of Glover Garden. He earned a Ph.D. in 2007 for research related to the former Nagasaki Foreign Settlement. He has published several books in Japanese and English, including *Starcrossed: A Biography of Madame Butterfly* (EastBridge, 2004) and *Nagasaki: The British Experience 1854-1945* (Global Oriental UK, 2009).

FLYING CRANE PRESS was established by the author in 2015 to publish information in various formats on the history and culture of the city of Nagasaki, Japan.

www.ingramcontent.com/pod-product-compliance
Lightning Source LLC
Chambersburg PA
CBHW061734020426
42331CB00006B/1242